Gender Ambiguity in
the Workplace

Gender Ambiguity in the Workplace

Transgender and Gender-Diverse Discrimination

Alison Ash Fogarty, PhD, and Lily Zheng

 PRAEGER™

An Imprint of ABC-CLIO, LLC

Santa Barbara, California • Denver, Colorado

Library of Congress Cataloging-in-Publication Data

Names: Fogarty, Alison Ash, author. | Zheng, Lily, author.
Title: Gender ambiguity in the workplace : transgender and gender-diverse
    discrimination / Alison Ash Fogarty, PhD, and Lily Zheng.
Description: Santa Barbara, California : Praeger, [2018] | Includes
    bibliographical references and index.
Identifiers: LCCN 2017054541 (print) | LCCN 2017058129 (ebook) |
    ISBN 9781440863233 (ebook) | ISBN 9781440863226 (hardcopy : alk. paper)
Subjects: LCSH: Transgender people—Employment. | Gender
    nonconformity. | Discrimination in employment. | Sex discrimination.
Classification: LCC HD6285 (ebook) | LCC HD6285 .F64 2018 (print) |
    DDC 331.5—dc23
LC record available at https://lccn.loc.gov/2017054541

ISBN: 978–1–4408–6322–6 (print)
      978–1–4408–6323–3 (ebook)

22 21 20 19 18   2 3 4 5

This book is also available as an eBook.

Praeger
An Imprint of ABC-CLIO, LLC

ABC-CLIO, LLC
130 Cremona Drive, P.O. Box 1911
Santa Barbara, California 93116-1911
www.abc-clio.com

This book is printed on acid-free paper ∞

Manufactured in the United States of America

Contents

Acknowledgments

First and foremost, we share our deep gratitude for the 25 individuals who participated in this research. The act of storytelling is a vulnerable one, and the openness and honesty with which these individuals shared their stories shook us to our core. This book would not be possible if not for their strength.

We are also grateful for the many research assistants who dedicated themselves to this project and the following funding organizations that made this research possible: the National Science Foundation Doctoral Dissertation Improvement Grant, Stanford Diversity Dissertation Research Opportunity Grant, Stanford Graduate Research Opportunities Fund, and the Stanford Sociology Research Opportunity Grant. And we'd like to thank Vanessa Sheridan for believing in this book and advocating on our behalf.

Alison: Paula England, Shelley Correll, and Cecilia Ridgeway, the years of guidance and insightful feedback you provided on this project was invaluable; thank you for your time and wisdom. Eden Williger, thank you for taking me to my first TDOR in 2008 and inspiring me to do this critical work. Kaiti Carpenter, thank you for working countless hours alongside me offering your generous encouragement; you fueled me more than you know. Tibet Sprague, thank you for the gift of true friendship; my life is so much better with you in it. And, finally, my parents, Dr. Gail Kaplan and Thomas Fogarty, thank you for instilling in me formative feminist beliefs and a passion for learning from an early age. I am so grateful for your unwavering support and unconditional love.

Lily: To my parents, thank you for teaching me to tell my own stories, and giving me the strength to write them down. To the activists in my life, thank you for sitting me down, raising me up, and showing me how to dream. To my partners and loved ones, thank you for the many long nights spent by my side, and for the words of encouragement along the way. Finally, to the trans people who have been my family, my inspiration, my grounding, and my light, thank you from the bottom of my heart. I am ever in awe of our community and its resilience.

Author's Note

As activists, we all have the little things we say to ourselves when we're back from the rallies, when we're tying our shoelaces, when we're filling water bottles or plugging in our laptop chargers in busy cafes. Small wishes, little rituals, our protest anthem to ourselves.

"I believe that we will win" was the one I learned.

When I was a young trans girl, I learned quickly that the world was not made for people like me. I had grown up on the same tired narratives that made trans people into slurs, punch lines, ghost stories, and boogeymen (or women, in my case), and as hard as I tried, I couldn't help but learn some of it. It didn't take me much longer to learn about the other things, about discrimination and marginalization, prejudice, and violence. "Why would you ever choose any of this?" people asked, and my response was always shame. I believed I deserved it.

Community gave me the hope to dream of a better world, and the strength to believe in the collective power of trans people and their allies. "I believe that we will win," I told myself, and saying it out loud gave those words power. I know now that the trans community is resilient, vibrant, loving, and fierce, and that the work of liberation—of dreaming up and moving toward a more just world where people of all identities and experiences can thrive—is larger than any of us. In writing this book, I am excited to play a part in this vision, and humbled by the work that has come before me. To the fighters, dreamers, survivors, and lovers who make up our global trans community, thank you. I believe that we will win.

Lily Zheng

Introduction

Those living on the fringes of society's gender norms have always been two steps ahead of academic efforts to catalog and categorize. Gender scholars have tried time and time again to document and explain the changing communities and identities throughout our world and have found themselves continuously surprised by what they discover. The groundbreaking theories that emerge from these stories may revolutionize academia, but these same ideas are old news to the communities who inspired them to begin with. For those communities who share their stories to researchers, academia may seem like an endless hole: greedily absorbing knowledge, transmuting it into the foreign language of theory, and then moving on, with little benefit to the communities this knowledge was extracted from.

As this is often a reality, so too is the fact that published research is often granted a high level of esteem in society, and drawn upon to inform real-world policies and practices. As academics push the boundaries of stored human knowledge forward, insights from research are disseminated, adapted, and implemented throughout the world. Rather than silence the voices of community, the potential exists for academics to be platforms for the marginalized narratives and experiences that are all too often concealed by society. In this book, interviews from 25 gender-diverse people, all of whom we refer to by pseudonyms to protect their anonymity, reveal rich insights into the nitty-gritty of life in the San Francisco Bay Area. These interviews were conducted by Dr. Alison Ash Fogarty between January 2012 and August 2013, and the interviewees whose stories made it into this book consented to have their words shared. As authors, we draw from these stories with a deep respect for the time and labor these individuals devoted to sharing their life experiences with us, and hope to do their narratives justice.

Gender is more than a passive topic of interest; it is an ongoing and active site of crisis and conflict in every society around the world. The recent explosion of transgender representation in media, pop culture, the fashion industry, and public understanding is grimly accompanied by the continuing murders of transgender people, particularly transgender women of color, the delegitimization of nonbinary identities, and pervasive and systemic exclusion from social, economic, and political life. Visibility for transgender communities has meant broader global awareness, but not yet broader global justice.

We write this book in the hopes that workplaces will change. We write this book with the understanding that we are not simply taking note of an ecological constant in the world, but standing at the cusp of the next waves of visibility and social justice. The experiences and narratives that form the core of this book are not unique to the California Bay Area; nor will they stay forever as only fringe voices at the edge of small but rapidly growing communities.

Our goals in writing this book are simple: we seek to humanize trans and gender-diverse people and communities as worthy of both academic study *and* three-dimensional portrayals, compassion, and justice. We intend this book to present a sorely needed challenge to existing transgender narratives, both inside and outside of academia, and to be a useful tool for advocacy and education alike. We hope that this book does justice by those individuals who volunteered their stories to us, and is able to create a better world for those whose stories have yet to be told. This book is our effort to help create a more just future in the ways we are able.

CHAPTER ONE

Transgender, Trans*, Trans

John Doe is just like every other guy at work. He does his job, is friendly with his coworkers, and talks occasionally about his wife and kids. Nothing much about him stands out, until one day he arrives at work with a new face, a new name, and a new body. Now John Doe is Jane Doe, now he is a she, now she is a woman when she once was a man. Jane Doe, as a transgender woman, must now face a series of mythically insurmountable challenges: her wife leaves her, taking their kids; she is fired from her workplace and starts a new life in a faraway city; her life becomes a constant struggle against discrimination, violence, isolation, and her own burgeoning sense of self.

This is but one of the many media-fueled transgender narratives in the United States, all related tales of body-switching, mystique, and suffering. These narratives are at best incomplete and at worst misleading. Whether in childhood, high school, employment, or intimacy, the real experiences of people who do not fit under society's default category of "men" and "women" are often packaged, repainted, and advertised as one-dimensional and voyeuristic stories. Those who challenge American society's notions of masculinity and femininity are thus seen as freaks, con artists and tragedies—not people deserving of love, support, or justice. Experiences of discrimination and ignorance become seen through this lens as worthy of pity but never policy—and so societal inequities persist unchallenged. Even in the realm of academia, discussion of gender-diverse people rarely deviates from similar one-dimensional narratives.

In this book, we examine the unique narratives of 25 gender-diverse peoples' workplace experiences navigating ignorance, harassment, and discrimination. Using qualitative analysis, we compare and contrast the discrimination experiences faced by the trans men, trans women, butch, nonbinary, and genderfluid people who shared their stories. These experiences and stories prompt many questions: How do discrimination experiences differ between different gender-diverse people? What might explain the observation that, while discrimination against gender-diverse people is almost universal, the appearance and outcomes of that discrimination vary immensely? What were some strategies gender-diverse people tried to avoid or reduce discrimination, and how well did they work?

This book includes a brief overview of transgender history, basic issues facing gender-diverse communities, and an overview of common terms to know. It follows up on this introduction with a deep dive into the discrimination experiences of our research participants and how they compare to what the academic literature on gender would predict. Finally, it ends with a succinct list of policy suggestions, drawing on insights from our original research to propose ways for organizations, managers, teams, and gender-diverse employees themselves to better survive and thrive in today's world.

THE HISTORY OF MODERN TERMINOLOGY AND CONCEPTS

In the last 50 years, the transgender community in the United States has profoundly shifted in terms of demographics, language usage, and definitions of identities. Different vocabulary has been used at different points in time by different groups of people for different social and political purposes. Understanding the current vocabulary and its current variations requires more than a simple laundry list of words and their dictionary definitions. Because the evolving language of transgender and gender-diverse people has always been tied to self-identity and community identity, language, history, and politics have forever been intertwined. For this reason, our dive into language 101 quickly becomes a journey into history, linguistics, and power.

For as long as the concept of "gender" has existed, so too have people and communities who did not conform to it. But even this simple statement hides a more complex reality. The history of the world has not been one in which any universal idea of "gender" has existed across all or even most nations, societies, or cultures. Notions of "manhood" and "womanhood"—and even the existence of such categories of *only* "men" and "women"—varied immensely across the globe and over time, with every culture and era having different conceptualizations of gender and its norms. One of these conceptualizations is that of the Judeo-Christian understanding of gender, in which men and women were distinct and differentiated into dominant roles for men and subservient roles for women. Women were expected to marry, and then bear and raise children, as well as attend to men, who were expected to lead the household, work, and provide for the family.

These are ideas that all modern readers around the world will recognize. But they have not always been universal. Many third genders in addition to "man" and "woman" have existed in societies around the world through history—the indigenous māhū of Hawai'i; the hijras of India, Pakistan, and Bangladesh; the femminielli of traditional Neapolitan culture; the kathoey of Thailand; and the mashoga of Kenya and Tanzania are examples. Even if specifically designated third genders didn't exist, many societies conceptualized the roles of "man" and "woman" in ways that blurred modern ideas of gender norms, like in the Kingdom of Dahomey, located in modern-day Benin, where a special regiment of unmarried and childless women fought as warriors; or in Edo-era Japan, where adolescent boys became *wakashu* as a stage before manhood, in which androgyny was celebrated and norms of sexuality and gender expression were loosened. These identities and expressions were seen as normative in some and as holding special spiritual or religious significance in others. Yet, this does not mean that all variations of gender identity and expression were celebrated. In Imperial China, for example, men and women were celebrated for dressing in clothing of the other gender for performance, yet those who chose to live in that role permanently faced heavy social and legal sanctions.

Time changed many of these things. As Christianity spread Judeo-Christian ideas of gender and gendered norms across Europe, religion became a standardizing force for gender across many different societies. And when these gendered ideas were conveyed by the missionaries and conquerors that served as colonization's vanguard, these Judeo-Christian conceptualizations of gender took root across the world—often times by force. Colonized societies adopted their colonizers' gender norms, and in this way, a "universal" conception of gender emerged out of these Judeo-Christian ideals. These burgeoning "universal" ideas about gender only strengthened in the 1900s and afterward, as modernization became a goal of many non-Western nations and the model of Western society became a thing to emulate. The formation of what institutional theorists would call a "global" or "world society" accelerated the standardization of many ideas, including hygiene, mass schooling, sexual norms, gender roles, and the gender binary. In relation to the now-universal Judeo-Christian ideas about gender, all past variation has become normatively "non-conforming."

It is with this backdrop of colonialism and Western-centrism that much of the language to understand gender diversity developed. In the early 1900s, the term "transvestite" was coined by sexologist Magnus Hirschfeld to describe men who frequently took on the clothing and/or mannerisms of women, and women who did so with the clothing and/or mannerisms of men. Gender-nonconformity under the term "transvestite" was simple for mainstream audiences to understand. The fact that this category aggregated gay men, lesbian women, straight cross-dressers of all genders, transgender women, transgender men, and other gender-nonconforming and gender-diverse people—though many of these labels had not yet been coined by these communities—did not matter.

In 1969, the Stonewall riots occurred in New York, and many self-identified transvestites, drag queens, gay men, transgender women, and other gender-diverse people who played a major role in this famous protest found themselves in the national spotlight. Organizations like Sylvia Rivera's Street Transvestite Action Revolutionaries formed in response to existing groups dominated by gay men and played a role in the increasing independence of communities organized around gender identity from those organized around sexual identity.

Sexologist Harry Benjamin, who created the Benjamin Scale in 1966 to determine if permission for sexual reassignment surgery should be granted for gender-diverse individuals, popularized the term *transsexual*. Benjamin described "transsexualism, with its demand for changes in the morphological structure of the body [as the] most severe form of gender role disorientation" (Benjamin 1969: 135). Benjamin focused on gender-diverse people who were assigned male at birth, and assigned special importance to genitalia. According to Benjamin, an individual who wears feminine clothing, no matter their commitment to their identity as a woman, is a transvestite until sexual reassignment surgery in which their penis is reshaped into a neo-vagina, at which point they become designated a "true" transsexual.

Yet, even at the time of Benjamin's writing, dissenting voices disagreed with this simplistic method of categorizing gender-diverse individuals. In 1968, Dr. Jan Wålinder established a set of criteria to eliminate the problem she saw: that "the line between transvestism and transsexualism drawn by many authors has been and still is too obscure" (1968: 255). The criteria she outlined for designation as a transsexual are listed below:

1. *A sense [sic] of belonging to the opposite sex, of having been born into the wrong sex, of being one of nature's extant errors.*
2. *A sense [sic] of estrangement with one's own body; all indications of sex differentiation are considered as afflictions and repugnant.*

3. *A strong desire to resemble physically the opposite sex via therapy including surgery.*
4. *A desire to be accepted by the community as belonging to the opposite sex.*

—Wålinder, "Transsexualism: Definition,
Prevalence and Sex Distribution" (1968: 255)

Wålinder was among the first to establish actual criteria for a gender-diverse identity situated not in some outside perception, but in an internal experience and self-identity. However, as a result of these criteria and their later dissemination into other literature, mass media narratives, and pop culture, transsexual identity became understood as not only based in self-identity, but also necessarily predicated on complete "estrangement from one's own body," a desire to be perceived as normative members of the "opposite" sex category than the one assigned at birth, and a desire to modify the body through any and all means available to achieve this goal. Thus, transsexual identity was constructed in a way that divorced itself from nonconforming gender expression and situated it alongside normative ideas of sex and gender as necessarily aligned and always binary. Transsexual women were seen as "nonconforming men" who wanted to be perceived as "normal women," and transsexual men were seen as "nonconforming women" who wanted to be perceived as "normal men." The terms MTF (male-to-female) and FTM (female-to-male) became the first colloquial designators for transsexual identity, and later adopted as medicalized terms describing particular regimens of hormone therapies, surgeries, and assorted services.

The history we have discussed so far has focused almost exclusively on the gender-nonconformity of those assigned male at birth (AMAB). However, the history of gender-nonconformity among those assigned female at birth (AFAB) is significant and substantive as well. Karl M. Baer, a German-Israeli writer and reformer, became one of the first AFAB individuals to gain full legal recognition as a man in 1907. In 1917, Dr. Joshua Gilbert became the first psychiatrist to recommend hysterectomy as a medical procedure solely to match a patient's gender identity. It is difficult, however, to differentiate the stories of women who presented themselves in stereotypically masculine ways, and women who identified as men.

Boyd (1999) describes a unique "tension" between lesbian communities, formed on the basis of sexual identity and attraction, and transgender communities, formed on the basis of gender identity and expression. She states "because of the relationship between butchness and lesbian sexuality, lesbian histories often conflate butch crossdressing (anatomical females sporting masculine appearance for the purpose of advertising lesbian sexuality) with female-to-male passing (anatomical females donning masculine appearance for the purpose of being perceived by others as men)" (74–75). Because of the many ways in which AFAB individuals in U.S. history have navigated masculinity, it is often difficult to separate out the experiences of AFAB individuals who "passed" as men out of desire for male privilege, in order to legitimize their love for women, or because they identified as men (Cromwell 1994; Duberman, Vicinus, and Chauncey 1989; Jones 1994; Katz 1976; Stryker 1995).

In the late 1960s, activists began using words like "transgenderal," "transgenderist," and "transgenderism" in an effort to create words that described individuals who experienced transitions of their gender identity and presentation without undergoing sex reassignment surgery or other permanent body modifications (Stryker 2008). In other words, they were looking to legitimize gender-diverse identities outside of the existing transsexual paradigm. In 1971, famous trans woman Christine Jorgensen identified herself in the media as "transgender," preferring the way the term drew focus to her gender identity instead of her sexuality. In 1991, activist Holly Boswell was among some of the first to use *transgender* as a term to encompass the entirety of gender-diverse experiences. By the early 1990s, transgender grew to have two commonly accepted meanings: one, an identity to describe in many ways the "transsexual" experience without the exacting criteria that had been used to define and medicalize the individual, and two, a unifying term seeking to welcome and include all experiences of marginalized gender identity.

Today, transgender is widely used as an umbrella term representing many identities. However, mainstream media tends to focus on those members of the transgender community who have a binary gender identity and pass as members of a binary sex category. This normalization of a particular image of what "transgender" is and should look like led some to push for more expansive language. By shortening the term "transgender" to "trans," for example, some communities have tried to subvert often convoluted and outdated language that uses the terms "transgender," "transgenders," "transgendered," and "transgenderism" interchangeably. Some communities have introduced and normalized the usage of "trans*," with the asterisk explicitly standing for nonbinary and genderfluid people and acknowledging that the mainstream transgender community is overrepresented by a particular transgender narrative (Tompkins 2014). Still others reject "trans*," claiming that the asterisk is a way of legitimizing the othering of nonbinary and genderfluid identities from the mainstream transgender narrative.

The last half-century has seen an explosion in transgender visibility, from media to academia to activism to popular culture. Transgender communities across the country have undergone rapid changes in response to the rapidly changing environment around them. As a result, we cannot simply conceptualize transgender identity as being defined only by the most recent wave of new language. In particular, many older members of transgender communities identify strongly with the identities of transsexual, transgender, MTF, and FTM. Younger trans people, on the other hand, are constantly introducing new vocabulary to describe their gender experiences and tend to identify with a wider range of identities, which we will further elucidate later in this chapter. The emergence of trans communities primarily comprising younger trans people has coincided with a new way of understanding gender that more explicitly critiques the gender binary, resulting in much exploration of nonbinary and genderfluid identities and expressions.

While many other terms would be appropriate, we have chosen to use the terms "trans" or "gender-diverse" throughout this book to refer to the extended family of identities that share in common a subversion of dominant gender norms. This is an intentionally broad definition, one that we leave broad in acknowledgment of the breadth and depth of the communities we study.

GENDER: A PRIMER

Transgender describes a number of non-normative gender identities and expressions that share a gender experience that does not conform to societal expectations of gender as binary and unchangeable and dictated by one's assigned sex at birth. Transgender as a term is often contrasted with the term *cisgender*, which describes an individual whose gender identity is fixed and aligned conventionally with their assigned sex at birth. In other words, people who identify as a boy and man (gender) and as male (sex at birth) or as a girl or woman (gender) and female (sex at birth) are cisgender. Truly understanding trans identity requires a thorough understanding of related but different concepts: biological sex, assigned sex at birth, gender essentialism, and the Western model's gender binary.

Biological Sex and Intersex

Biological sex, which is believed to be innate and unchangeable, is also assumed to be binary and mutually exclusive, meaning a person must be either male or female and cannot be neither or both. However, closer scrutiny of the idea reveals a lack of consensus from the scientific community on just what exactly constitutes a male or female. If it is genitalia, then castrated males would hypothetically become sexless; if it is chromosomes, individuals who are born with XXY chromosomes theoretically could not be sex categorized; if it is reproductive ability, individuals who have had a hysterectomy hypothetically would no longer be females; if it is hormone levels, then a great number of those who consider themselves females must hypothetically be male—as many females have higher levels of testosterone than males. So many exceptions exist to whatever rules constructed to define biological sex that we can reasonably conclude that no universal definition is readily available (Herdt 1994).

In 1955, a series of studies done at John Hopkins Hospital in Baltimore, Maryland, on *intersex* individuals—individuals whose genitalia, physiology, or other characteristics do not match up with binary notions of "biological sex"—led to the conclusion that sex was a label that could be (re)assigned. John Money and his colleagues concluded sex needed to be assigned as either male or female in an effort to maximize the baby's ability to properly function in society, focusing on reproductive ability and overall psychological well-being (Money, Hampson, and Hampson 1955). Existing paradigms in the medical community strongly shaped the prioritization of these goals, and continue to set the standards by which sex is still assigned today.

That John Money and his colleagues prioritized reproductive ability as a key aspect of societal functioning is no coincidence. Reproduction as a societal good emerged in no small part due to perceptions of reproduction as a biological mandate, an ideal promulgated by Charles Darwin. Darwin, in his examination of reproduction in animal species, theorized that the purpose of sexual dimorphism—the differentiation of "males" and "females" of a species—is procreation, and that genitalia were the primary means by which this reproduction takes place. Darwin advocated strongly for the idea that humans too are sexually dimorphic, fundamentally and biologically organized into "male" and "female," with differentiated genitalia evolved for the purpose of reproduction. This seemingly elegant solution took hold in the scientific community, and sexual dimorphism has been the norm since Darwin's time. As a result, biological or physiological variation has been viewed as an "abnormality" or "disorder," contraception became an impediment to the natural outcome of sexual intercourse, and same-sex intimate partnerships become vilified as flouting the "essential" order of the biological world.

Intersex people may vary on the number or type of sex chromosomes, number of ovaries or testicles, estrogen or testosterone levels, internal reproductive anatomy, and/or external genitalia. However, of all these potential sites of variation, only two are relied upon for sex assignment: reproductive anatomy and external genitalia. Fausto-Sterling, in *Sexing the Body* (2000), describes the guidelines for sex assignment, which state that "genetic females should always be raised as females, preserving reproductive potential . . . in the genetic male, however, the gender of assignment is based on the infant's anatomy, predominantly the size of the phallus" (57). Babies born with an organ deemed too small to ever be able to adequately penetrate as a penis are often assigned to be females through a complex series of procedures often involving surgery, hormone monitoring and treatments, and a mixture of therapy and "psychosocial" rearing of the child. The underlying assumption is almost always that an individual's happiness and ability to function in society depends on there being an unambiguous match between genitalia, sex, and gender, and that "corrective" treatments are always in the individual's best interests—even when the individual in question is scarcely a day out of the womb and unable to consent (Dreger 1998).

Colloquial usage of the term "sex" often makes no mention of it as an assigned characteristic at birth and rarely acknowledges the border between male and female as socially constructed. Most often, "sex" is used as shorthand for the term *sex category*: a descriptor for either of two perceived preexisting groups, male and female. *Sex categorization*, or the assignment of an individual into a sex category, is an automatic activity that people take part in upon interaction (Blair and Banaji 1996; Brewer and Lui 1989; Stangor et al. 1992). People often rely on other's secondary sex characteristics, including presence of breasts, facial hair, voice pitch, size of hands and feet, hip-to-waist ratio, and muscle mass, as well as their gender expression, including hair style, style of dress, and mannerisms, as cues when engaging in sex categorization. The factors that cause us to categorize each other as "male" or "female" are not solely attributes of biological sex, but also expression of gender, which then lead us to make assumptions about genitalia, assigned sex at birth, and gender identity. If we run into a stranger whom we sex categorize as female, we assume that this individual has a vulva and uterus, has XX chromosomes, identifies as a woman, and uses she/her pronouns. If we run into a stranger whom we sex categorize as male, we assume that this person has a penis and two testicles, has XY chromosomes, identifies as a man, and uses he/him pronouns.

Gender and Transgender

Ridgeway and Correll (2004) describe *gender* as an "institutionalized system of social practices for constituting people as two significant different categories, men and women, and organizing social relations of inequality on the basis of that difference" (510). In other words, the gender binary is created and recreated on every level of society, from how children are taught gendered behavior and recreate it to how larger communities, organizations, and societal institutions reproduce and reinforce the separation of man and woman.

Individuals are raised with the understanding that men and women correspond not only to penises and vulvas, but also to blue and pink, and assertiveness and passivity, tuxedos and dresses. From our first moments in this world as children, the system of gender is placed onto us—in this way, we can think of not only sex but gender as something that is assigned at birth. Gendered differences are taught and reproduced through a complex and enduring system of gender socialization and behavioral policing at the interactional level and pressure from institutions in society, including the family, scientific-medical community, education system, and media.

Gender identity describes an individual's subjective understanding of their own gender experience constructed into a self-identity. Gender identity refers not only to the gender label people assign themselves, but also to each person's understanding of what that label means. In this way, it is possible for two individuals with the same gender identity to have very different conceptualizations of the meanings of that identity

Our society is constructed with strong cultural tendencies to assume that gender identity is binary and always corresponds to assigned sex at birth. In other words, babies who are assigned a male sex at birth are assumed to grow to identify as a boy and then later as a man. Babies who are assigned a female sex at birth are assumed to grow to identify as a girl and later as a woman. Everyone is assumed to be *cisgender*—to identify as the sex and gender they were assigned at birth.

Socially defined feminine or masculine characteristics, mannerisms, items, and occupations exist separately from an individual's self-identity. In fact, although society constantly glorifies the hypermasculine man—agentic, dominant, strong, intelligent, conventionally attractive, heterosexual, and virile,—and the hyperfeminine women—communal, dependent, docile, alluring, conventionally attractive, heterosexual, and fertile—the vast majority of individuals in society fail to meet these prototypical definitions. Gender identity is constructed often in acknowledgment of gender expectations, but almost never fully conforms to prescriptive stereotypes. The idea that gender identity exists *independent* of assigned sex and gender at birth is prominent in most trans individuals' conception of self-identity. That is, trans men often identify as men and trans women often identify as women regardless of their assigned sex at birth.

Because gender identity is *not* solely inherent, individual gender identity must also be affirmed in interactions with others. Its legitimacy is necessarily affected by social perception. In other words, an AFAB man must have his identity as a man validated by the world around him in order for that identity to hold social legitimacy. For trans people, this societal legitimation of their gender identity is often of high importance. For this reason, while Ridgeway and Correll define "gender" as "almost always a background identity ... [which] operates as an implicit, cultural/cognitive presence that colors people's activities in varying degrees but that is rarely the ostensible focus of what is going on in the situation" (2004: 516), we argue that trans people often interact with gender identity in the foreground of their consciousness.

In order to have their gender identity recognized and validated by society, individuals often must have a *gender expression* that matches their gender identity. This gender expression is often a means by which individuals "do gender," a concept that West and Zimmerman originally describe in their seminal piece by the same name published in 1987 as "a situated doing ... an emergent feature of social situations: both as an outcome of and a rationale for various social arrangements and as a means of legitimating one of most fundamental divisions of society" (1987: 126). Gender expression is more than an action made to satisfy personal identity; it is a bridge between the self and society, a way of performing a personal identity for the outside world.

Gender expression is a means by which gender can be displayed and performed—dresses, makeup, and crossed legs are all forms of gender expression that perform femininity; business suits, facial hair, and expansive body posture are all forms of gender expression that perform masculinity. Gender expression is not limited to outward displays like clothing or behavioral mannerisms. Physical characteristics such as shoulder and ribcage width, facial bone structure, and size of hands and feet, along with secondary sex characteristics, including breast shape and facial hair, also carry gendered associations. While many of these characteristics are not "performed" in the same way that gendered behavioral mannerisms are, there are many ways to alter these physical expressions of gender. Makeup can be used for facial contouring to give the appearance of more masculine or

feminine bone structure; padding can be used to simulate more feminine breasts and hips; chest binders can be used to compress breasts
to give the appearance of a flat chest. Surgeries are also options for
modifying these physical characteristics, giving individuals more control over their expression of gender. *Transitioning* can be described as a
series of steps a person can take toward a more genuine gender identity or expression. This can describe an internal transition, focused on
internal changes to gender identity, a social transition, focused on
changing outside perceptions of gender identity, or a physical transition, focused on changes to physiology or gender expression.

The interaction between gender identity, gender expression, and
gendered expectations demonstrates the highly variable nature of
trans identity. Gendered expectations act on both gender identity and
gender expression by establishing a baseline for self-identification
and personal construction of an authentic gender expression. At the
heart of this interaction is the concept that identity and expression
are determined by the self—an individual who self-identifies as a
woman may in fact reject societal beliefs concerning womanhood; an
individual who describes their gender expression as feminine may in
fact reject societal beliefs concerning femininity. It is the act of existing
in a social world, however, that necessitates doing gender in order to
legitimate self-identity. Those clashing intersections of self-identity
and outside labeling—for example, an individual who self-identifies
as a man who is labeled by others to be a woman—embody the difficulties many trans people face on a daily basis.

Passing

Passing is used to describe the successful categorization during
interpersonal interaction of a trans individual into a normative gender
group, usually accomplished through intentionally shaping a gender
expression conducive to the desired sex categorization. A trans person
who passes as a cisgender woman would be perceived as a woman on
the basis of characteristics like voice, hair, clothing, verbal and behavioral mannerisms, and accessories. Passing often draws not only on
societal ideas about what it means to be a man or a woman, but also
intersects with societal ideas about race and age. For example, passing
as a young black man involves a different set of categorical rules compared to passing as an older, white man.

In many trans communities, passing is a goal: being perceived and
treated as a cisgender man or woman is for many people the primary
motivation to modify gender expression, and for some the primary
motivation to transition. Passing is an either/or designation; an

individual either passes or doesn't. Trans communities, particularly communities of trans women and trans femmes, have developed an extensive lexicon to describe the many outcomes associated with passing. Trans people who do not pass are said to be *read* or *clocked* as trans and are often *misgendered*, or referred to with the incorrect language or gender pronouns. Calling a trans woman a "man," referring to her as "manly," and using the pronoun "he" are all examples of misgendering. Perhaps in recognition of the difficulties that nonpassing trans people experience, many trans communities that utilize the language of passing, reading, and clocking also engage in community efforts to critique, comment on, or offer tips to trans people who do not pass, with the intent of helping them do so.

While many trans people make significant efforts to pass to lower their discomfort with their appearances, bodies, or gender presentations, there is also significant motivation from society to pass. Being perceived as gender-nonconforming may negatively affect interpersonal relations, intimate pursuits, and workplace experiences. For this reason, some trans people who are able to pass as cisgender often choose to hide their trans identities and history—go *stealth*—in order to avoid the discrimination and prejudice experienced by nonpassing trans people. Stealth often refers to intentional efforts on the part of a trans person to pass as cisgender, and be perceived, treated, and interacted with accordingly. While stealth tends to refer to a specific environment or situation in which a trans identity is hidden or not made salient, *deep stealth* describes a situation in which an individual is stealth to virtually every person they know within all conceivable domains in their life. Often, these individuals have taken significant social and medical efforts to pass successfully and seek to blend back into society, no longer seen as trans.

While going stealth or deep stealth may lead to significant improvements in quality of life, trans people, especially those in deep stealth, often experience fatigue from constantly working to maintain their stealth status (Meyer 2003). Hiding a past trans identity requires significant amounts of physical work, including dealing with the governmental bureaucracy in an effort to modify all identifying documents as well as the cognitive energy expended in the careful monitoring of gendered behaviors, actions, and activities. Concealing a stigmatized identity causes notable psychological distress, and is linked with worse health outcomes in the long term (Quinn and Chaudoir 2009).

Up to this point, we have explained concepts in relation to communities trans men and trans women. However, trans experiences are often far more complicated than AMAB people identifying as women and AFAB people identifying as men. While many people who identify as trans do choose to identify as a man or a woman, others identify with a variety of nonbinary gender identities.

Nonbinary

Nonbinary people face a set of problems at once both similar and strikingly different from those faced by binary-identifying trans people. While binary-identifying trans people often describe themselves as simply moving from one end of the gender binary to the other, nonbinary trans people instead choose to situate themselves in between or outside of the binary all together. Because society is so invested in the gender binary, those who defy binary conceptions of gender can face societal exclusion due to their rejection of what is thought of as a fundamental and unquestionable identity. The difficulties that come from simultaneously existing as a social actor in the world and rejecting the basic social framework of gender are immense.

Some nonbinary people today identify as *genderqueer*, a word that Heather Love describes as "the refusal of all categories of sexual and gender identity" (2014: 173). Used as early as 1995, in Riki Anne Wilchins's "In Your Face," published in the spring newsletter of *Transsexual Menace*, the term "genderqueer" as an identity has since proliferated widely through communities of alternative sexual and gender identities (Stryker 2008). In the 2002 anthology *GenderQueer*, Riki Wilchins describes the adoption of the term "Gender Queer" in response to a perceived failure of the intended umbrella term of "transgender" to include narratives outside the experiences of trans men and women or otherwise binary-identified, medically transitioning identities (Nestle, Howell, and Wilchins 2002). Today, the term "genderqueer" continues to function both as an umbrella identity encompassing nonbinary gender identities and as a stand-alone identity. In both contexts, it has become a unifying term that has been adopted by many gender-diverse people and communities.

While we have described gender up to this point as intersecting along the axes of identity, expression, and perception, gender also varies for many people as a function of time. Our society readily accepts the idea that for all individuals their perception of their gender identity changes across the life course. A young boy's understanding of his gender identity is not the same as his understanding of it as a teenager, nor is it the same when he grows to be an elderly man. We have complicated this narrative so far by suggesting that perhaps an AFAB infant may later grow to identify as a woman or as a nonbinary individual. However, implying that this is the extent to which gender may change is drastically oversimplifying the concept.

Gender identity, like all identities, can change multiple times over the course of an individual's life. The adoption of a new identity does not negate the legitimacy of previous ones, despite the popular saying that past identities were "just a phase." When these changes occur on a short timescale, say, weeks, days, or even hours, individuals may identify as *genderfluid*. Genderfluid individuals may experience their gender identity as fluid, in flux, or varying over time. Their gender identities may vary between any combination of binary or nonbinary identities. Some genderfluid people feel that their identities shift for no discernible reason, while others find that their gender identities are influenced by their environment, situation, or personal desires. Genderfluid identity often intersects with genderqueer identity in a number of ways. Some genderfluid people may view their gender-fluidity itself as a form of subversive genderqueerness, while others may fluctuate into a genderqueer identity as one of the various gender identities that comprise their genderfluid experience. Others may fluctuate only between binary genders and not identify their gender fluidity as genderqueer at all.

Given this broad overview of gender diversity within the "trans" umbrella, is there a parsimonious way to define what it means to be "trans"? We choose to define "trans" in its simplest form as:

> Self-identified deviation from normative gendered identities, bodies, or experiences.

Trans cannot be boiled down to a stable identity or set of identities, nor can it be understood as a group defined easily by a simple set of characteristics. While some trans people identify as outside the gender binary, many do not. While some trans people's bodies differ from the binary norm, many's do not. And clearly, while many trans people's stories share similarities, just as many have experiences and narratives unlike those of any others.

Understanding the spectrum of trans people's identities and experiences requires reevaluating commonly held ideas about the gender binary, gender essentialism, and identity politics. Judith Butler, in *Bodies That Matter* (1993), writes that "if the term 'queer' is to be a site of collective contestation . . . it will have to remain that which is, in the present, never fully owned, but always and only redeployed, twisted, queered from a prior usage and in the direction of urgent and expanding political purposes." Just as the queering of identity defies definition, so too does the constantly evolving cornucopia of trans identities, bodies, and experiences defy boundaries. Among our interviewees, we could see this immediately in how definitions of the same term varied immensely. It rings true that the boundaries of being "trans" lie only in the boundaries of our imaginations, and in the possibilities of human experience.

THE PEOPLE YOU'LL MEET IN THIS BOOK

The people whose stories are featured in this book were interviewed in 2012 and 2013, and all worked and lived in the San Francisco Bay Area at the time of the interviews. They identified as butch, trans, female, FTM trans, trans male, transmasculine, masculine presenting female, female prince, andro, male-leaning androgyn, masculine of center, genderqueer, gender-neutral, genderfluid, male, gender-anomalous, gender-variable, agender, genderless, and transcending gender. Some people described their gender identity using two or more of these labels, which, along with the extensive variety of labels given, highlights the complexity of people's understanding of their own gender identity and expression. Five of these participants used he/him pronouns, eight used she/her pronouns, and the remaining used either gender-neutral pronouns, no pronouns, or some other combination of gender pronouns at the time of the interviews. Throughout this book, we refer to people using the gender identity and pronouns (or lack of pronouns) that participants used in their social lives, even if they were referred to by different pronouns at their places of employment.

None of our interviewees had a gender expression that was static, nor did their gender expression necessarily move in a linear pattern from masculine to feminine or vice versa during transition. Our book focuses on gender ambiguity because of the insights that we saw in our interviewees' experiences of being perceived as an ambiguously gendered person in the world. While some participants had an ambiguous gender expression at the time of the interview and others did not, all could reflect and share about a period of their life when they identified or were perceived as ambiguous. For many of our participants, ambiguity occurred as a transient period created by medical transition, hormone replacement treatment (HRT) and other physical and medical procedures. For others, ambiguity occurred as a middle stage in social transition, as participants experimented with padding, binders, makeup, and mannerisms to change how they were perceived in the world. For still others, ambiguity was the explicit objective of transition, and was carefully maintained and created through medical means, social means, or a mix of both.

In order to protect the privacy of these interviewees, we have changed their names and withheld the names of the companies where they have worked. Participants range from 21 to 60 years of age. Nineteen of these participants identify as white, four identify as Hispanic or Latinx, one identifies as Asian American, and one identifies as indigenous. Two of these participants have a high school diploma or GED, three had some college education, six have an associate's degree, twelve have a bachelor's degree, and two have a graduate degree. We have fifteen participants who earned less than $40,000 a year, seven participants who earned between $40,000 and $80,000, and eight participants who earned over $80,000.

In this book, we have chosen to use the umbrella term *trans* rather than transgender in an attempt to include people with a wide range of non-normative gender identities and experiences. However, because many of our interviewees do not identify with the term "trans," we also use the umbrella term *gender-diverse* to describe the larger communities of transgender, gender-nonconforming, gender-variant, and intersex people. When referring to specific individuals, we use the identity or identities they provide. While some of these participants define their gender identity as "male" or "female," which we appropriately quote and include, in our prose we additionally use "assigned female at birth" or "AFAB" and "assigned male at birth" or "AMAB" when referring to sex assignment at birth. We use these words to explicitly call attention to the constructed nature of the binary sex categories "male" and "female." In addition, we use "woman" and "man" when referring to gender identity and "feminine" and "masculine" when referring to gender expression. We make these important distinctions to better separate the ideas of biological sex and gender, which are almost always conflated in our society.

Finally, we have categorized the gender-diverse people interviewed for this book into five categories so as to more meaningfully discuss the similarities behind them. Any process of categorization, however, necessarily loses some of the preciseness of the original terms people used to define themselves. We identify this decision as an intentional compromise made to better help us analyze and present the themes we saw, and not as any indication that as authors we have any authority to decide on the identities of those people we interviewed.

The categories with their participants are as follows:

Trans Women and Trans Femmes	Trans Men and Transmasculine	Butch Women	Assigned Male at Birth Nonbinary/ Genderfluid	Assigned Female at Birth Nonbinary Genderfluid
Alex	Blake	Pat	Casey	Cameron
Kelly	Brett	Sam	Hayden	Cory
Leslie	Cassidy		Jordan	Jessie
Robin	Drew		Lee	Rory
Taylor	Kai		Phoenix	Rowan
Whitney	Parker			
	Sawyer			

CHAPTER TWO

Narratives of Trans Discrimination

The workplace experiences of our participants were many and varied over a wide range of industries, management levels, and workplace cultures. Every interviewee we spoke to could speak to at least one employment experience in which conflict—tied to their trans or gender-diverse status—was salient. In this chapter, we follow the complex narratives of our cohort of 25 trans and gender-diverse interviewees from the time of their first employment in the San Francisco Bay Area.

In our interviews, we asked participants to speak about experiences of discrimination they faced in any of their workplaces. While some of the stories we heard—stories of violence, harassment, and derogatory language—constituted clear and obvious instances of prejudice and discrimination, many others were more difficult to assess. The stories we heard about bias, preference, neglect, and exclusion are among this gray area: we cannot confirm these stories without interviewing the coworkers, hiring officers, and managers our participants felt discriminated by. Even then, there is no guarantee that these interviews would reveal the true motivations or thought processes present at the time of the perceived discrimination.

With this in mind, we strove to take each and every story of discrimination at face value, recognizing that whether or not an intention or motivation to discriminate was present, our participants nevertheless felt the real psychological and emotional effects of discrimination. Whenever possible, we draw from information participants provided to us to infer as much as we can about the motivations and contexts in which discrimination takes place, and take note of the explanations that participants themselves provided. We thus make our best effort to piece together the subjective truth of gender-diverse discrimination, acknowledging that the perception of the same situations would have appeared differently to the unaffiliated eyewitness, the individual(s) accused of discrimination, and to us as social scientists. Our major hypotheses about the factors behind perceived discrimination—the motivations and contexts at the heart of our participants' stories—can be found in Chapters Three and Four.

TRANS WOMEN AND TRANS FEMMES

Alex

Alex, a white trans woman in her forties who uses she/her pronouns, has been searching for employment during the entirety of her time in the Bay Area.

As an executive at a multinational computer corporation where she had worked for more than ten years, coming to terms with her trans identity was difficult. The experience of a trans colleague whose career stagnated after transitioning dissuaded her from transitioning on the job, so Alex resolved instead to make subtle changes at work, changing her management style and beginning to grow out her hair and nails. Her colleagues quickly picked up the new changes. "It took one day at work before I cut them and swore to myself I would never allow them to grow," Alex explained.

Alex quit her job and moved to San Francisco, where she began her medical transition and hunted for employment. However, she has been unsuccessful in her interviews so far, identifying that her lower voice gives away her trans identity. Alex is certain that she is being discriminated against. In a conversation with a headhunter and recruiter, she was told, "Don't bother going through any recruiters, because they're not going to touch you."

"You know," Alex remarked, "if that's the case I'm just going to have to adjust my expectations of what I can contribute." At the time of the interview, Alex was still job-hunting.

Kelly

Kelly, a white trans woman in her sixties who uses she/her pronouns, transitioned four years before her interview and worked as a freelance architect.

Despite Kelly's impressive expertise and work experience after decades of work, she has been largely unable to find clients after transitioning. Many clients have refused to hire Kelly upon knowing of Kelly's trans identity out of the fear that associating with Kelly will damage their own reputation. One employer said to her, "You're a transsexual, you're going to kill this job for me if I take you to [stakeholders]." Another employer refused to hire Kelly out of the fear that his customers would say, "You brought a guy in a dress." "They think of me as a guy pretending to be a woman," Kelly explained. "Clients don't want to be associated with me."

The financial implications of this discrimination have been tremendous on Kelly, and she summed up her situation well when she frankly stated, "I've made maybe five grand in two years . . . people don't hire transsexuals." When asked why, Kelly was equally blunt in her response. "If [employers] got a choice, why take the queer when you got a perfectly good something else?"

Leslie

Leslie, a white trans woman in her thirties who uses she/her pronouns, was working in the same biotech company where she transitioned many years earlier at the time of the interview.

Leslie's transition experience has been surprisingly straightforward compared to others interviewed. She set up a meeting with her company's HR, and began going through the steps of a previously established workplace transition routine. "It was phenomenal," she said. When Leslie encountered confusion from others in her facility, HR stepped in to fight on her behalf by organizing mandatory workshops and providing information to employees.

The bulk of Leslie's discrimination has consisted of offensive comments made by ignorant coworkers, many of whom Leslie took the initiative to educate. On the whole, Leslie's workplace experiences were overwhelmingly positive—though as a result of being the only out trans woman in this company, she felt increased pressure at times to be a perfect role model. At the time of her interview, she was serving a leadership role in the company's LGBT Employee Resource Group that started her on her path to transition.

Robin

Robin, a white trans woman in her fifties who uses she/her pronouns, began her social and medical transition three years prior to her interview. At the time of the interview, she worked as an audio technician in a labor union, where she has worked for most of her professional career and transitioned on the job.

Robin was the first out trans person in the history of her union, and at the time of her transition, no nondiscrimination policy existed. Robin's supervisor, while initially supportive of her transition, misgendered Robin for weeks on end. When Robin eventually told him in no uncertain terms to "get it right," he retaliated by badmouthing Robin to the union and restricting her from work. As Robin explained, "Prior to this incident, I earned $20,000 a year in that building. I earn $1,000 now."

The few gigs that Robin has received since this incident have often subject her to discrimination. In one gig, a security guard accosted her and accused her of being a man in the women's bathroom. At another, a religious stagehand told Robin that she would "burn in hell" for being a "cross-dresser." All things considered, Robin has been able to transition at work and successfully keep her job. However, while Robin was one of the most senior and experienced union members, she was no longer given as challenging, high-paying, or as many jobs, and the work that she did do was overscrutinized and micromanaged. Robin briefly remarked on how, before her transition, she knew she made more money than a woman coworker with equivalent experience and expertise. After her transition, however, she made far less.

Taylor

Taylor, a white trans woman in her thirties who uses she/her pronouns, moved to San Francisco in her early thirties to transition and begin hormone therapy.

Looking for employment as a trans woman, for Taylor, felt like "starting over." Her first job, for example, was at an entry-level position at an LGBT hotel that left her underpaid but supported in her identity, a workplace that she describes as a "sanctuary." At the time of her interview, she was working two jobs. The first was a teaching position at a Jewish school, a place where Taylor's trans identity made a big splash when she was first hired. Taylor tells a story about how one day after class, "a parent calls me over as if I'm trying to corrupt [their child] . . . I had to sit there and explain for ten minutes that [gendered nouns are] part of Hebrew." Over the past three years, the school community slowly grew more comfortable with her. Her other job was a youth counselor at a hospital facility, where the troubled youth she worked with were far less supportive. The lack of established trans-inclusive policies for employees, additionally, caused Taylor anxiety. It wasn't clear if Taylor, who was out in that workplace as a trans woman, would be allowed to take shifts in the girl's wing. "I'm scared to hear what I don't want to hear," Taylor admitted.

Taylor was frank about how her employment experiences have changed after transitioning. Despite her best efforts, she explained, "In all my jobs I've gone down in salary instead of up."

Whitney

Whitney, a white trans woman in her twenties who uses she/her pronouns, was unemployed and attempting to pick up software engineering after several years working in manufacturing when she was interviewed.

Whitney's discrimination experiences began when she started growing out her hair and experimenting with eyeliner at a machine shop. "While I was there," Whitney explained, "my supervisor started hassling me about my presentation, the length of my hair . . . I was starting to get giggles and stuff because I wear light eyeliner and a little bit of makeup." Whitney observed that as she began presenting more feminine in the workplace, she garnered less and less respect. Six months into the job, Whitney started the medical transition process and began HRT. A week later, she was fired.

Because of the nature of manufacturing work, Whitney was no stranger to leaving and applying for new jobs in the industry. After more than a year of job-hunting, however, she was still without a manufacturing job despite experimenting with varying her name and clothing during interviews. Whitney's continued joblessness, especially in an industry she has so much experience with, has had a significant emotional impact on her. She told us, "My confidence is just broken." As a result of her unemployment, Whitney began to seek skills in software engineering at a local LGBT center. For Whitney, the most promising path ahead was one which took her far away from the manufacturing industry she spent most of her career in.

TRANS MEN AND TRANSMASCULINE

Brett

Brett, a white trans man in his twenties, began transitioning seven years before his interview and uses he/him pronouns. In the San Francisco Bay Area, he has worked in the food service, nonprofit, education, and customer service industries.

Brett came out to his coworkers for the first time at a customer service job. However, after he came out, his coworkers continued referring to him with she/her pronouns, as well as feminine pet names like "little mama." This experience made Brett less comfortable with being out at work, and so at his next jobs, he kept his trans identity under wraps.

At an elementary school, Brett worried that "parents [would] assume that there was inherently something sexual to [being trans]" and that this would strain the parent–teacher relationship.

At a women's health nonprofit, he similarly chose not to disclose his trans identity to better identify with the women he worked with. And in another job at a rape crisis services nonprofit, Brett feared that identifying as a man would have impacted his ability to connect with the victims. "I'd wanted to be out as male, but . . . a lot of the women faced assault from men and I didn't feel like I was creating a safe space for others." Brett explains, "I feel like my identity for a long time was dictated by the environment that I was in."

Brett eventually found himself in a period of unemployment, and sought out the help of the Trans Employment Program, a program run by the San Francisco LGBT Center. This program was eventually able to secure Brett a job doing vocational work, where he had recently begun employment at the time of the interview.

Parker

Parker, a white trans man in his twenties, uses he/him pronouns and began socially and medically transitioning one year before his interview. At the time of the interview, he was still working as a sales analyst at the workplace where he transitioned on the job one year earlier.

The bulk of Parker's discrimination experiences occurred before he transitioned, when he was perceived to be a butch woman. Before transitioning at his sales analyst job, Parker experienced alienation and exclusion from both men's and women's workplace networks. "I would kind of sit somewhere in the middle . . . and that was kind of othering in that way." While Parker's more masculine presentation was accepted in the office, his coworkers occasionally pressured him to dress in more feminine wear to travel abroad, a compromise he was unwilling to make.

A year before the interview, Parker began identifying as a trans man and transitioned at work with the help of HR. When he returned— using a new masculine name and he/him pronouns—it was like he had joined a different workplace. "Probably the most stark difference, and I didn't necessarily expect it, was that I was instantly in the boys club," Parker explained. As a result of Parker's newfound privilege, his workplace prospects greatly improved. "I still have the same job title but my responsibilities have grown. I think they were very related to gender changes and the way that I'm viewed with the company . . . I have had several promotions in the last year, pay raises, and a lot more opportunity to explore more things." For Parker, transitioning on the job dramatically improved his workplace experience.

Blake

Blake, a mixed white and Jamaican American trans man in his twenties, began his social transition ten years before his interview and his medical transition two years before the interview. Blake has received discrimination across many different jobs and workplaces, though the nature of this discrimination has changed as Blake's gender identity and gender expression have shifted over time.

While working for an LGBT nonprofit, Blake was aggressively teased about his sexuality, his size, and his gender expression until he was forced to quit. A coworker told him to "man up" after seeing him struggle to lift a heavy object, while another bluntly told him to "do something with those boobs." At a video game company, Blake was consistently passed over for promotions and was forced to train several new hires who were promoted over him during his time there. When a transphobic general manager joined the workplace and discovered that Blake was trans, Blake became the target of derisive and transphobic jokes and was forced to quit this position as well.

At his current place of employment doing shipment work, Blake faced teasing targeting his small size, lack of physical strength, and trans identity. Still, Blake was grateful to this last job for giving him a working environment with few people to harass him. "I was an unloader. So, you talk to your supervisor [when] you clocked in. They told you which trucks were yours and you did your work. And you didn't really work with anybody."

"It was ideal," Blake added.

Kai

Kai, a white transmasculine person in his thirties who uses he/him pronouns, began medically transitioning seven years before his interview. Kai recently moved to California, where he works at a veterinary practice.

While Kai's current job was in California, the majority of his work experience has been from working in Arizona. At a veterinary ophthalmology clinic early on in Kai's work history, Kai decided to start masculinizing HRT. As soon as Kai told his supervisor, however, he began to face extreme discrimination. "He basically made my entire life hell at work. He treated me like a piece of shit." Kai's supervisor took actions that included demoting Kai, slashing his pay, restricting his continuing education opportunities, and giving him an unmanageable work schedule. Kai tried going to human resources, but when his representative made a fuss on Kai's behalf, Kai's boss had the representative replaced. Without the support of nondiscrimination laws in that company or that state, Kai was eventually forced to quit for his own safety.

From this point onward, Kai was unabashed about his trans identity while job searching, even with mismatching ID cards that often led to hiring discrimination. The few jobs that Kai was able to secure were rife with name-calling, insults, harassment, and blatant wage discrimination. Kai felt treated, in his words, "like a leper." It was at this point that Kai decided to move to California in search of employment where he could be out as trans, and eventually found a job at a hospice company. At this workplace, Kai's immediate supervisor bars Kai from talking about gender or sexuality with his patients, a missive that Kai routinely ignores. Being in California has given Kai a new opportunity to embrace an authentic gender identity and carry on the advocacy work that is so important to him.

Cassidy

Cassidy, an Asian American transmasculine person in their twenties who uses they/them pronouns, began medically transitioning two years before the interview and worked as a legal consultant at the time of the interview.

As Cassidy started their medical transition, they began working as a biotech consultant. As Cassidy's voice began to deepen and their gender expression became perceived as more masculine, they noticed that people at this workplace saw them less as a butch woman, and more as a gay man. The homophobia they faced convinced Cassidy to keep their trans identity private. "People were really mean to me as far as just being gay, just being gay alone and I think like being trans would have like blown their brains apart."

As their medical transition continued, Cassidy decided to embrace consulting and largely take a break from 9-to-5 employment until they felt comfortable with themselves. At one consulting job, Cassidy felt like their supervisor discouraged them from taking phone calls with clients due to the high pitch of their voice. At the other firm, in contrast, Cassidy's supervisor took the lead on including Cassidy and validating their transmasculine identity. "He would say to the other associate attorneys like, 'Oh, this is Cassidy. *He's* doing this' and so people would follow his lead."

The importance of this seemingly small act of inclusion was not lost on Cassidy. "I think," he elaborated, "people made it a really plushy place for me to just go ahead and just be me."

Sawyer

Sawyer, a white trans man in his twenties, has been on and off masculinizing HRT since his teens, stopping usage mainly to avoid unwanted side effects. Sawyer worked as a sex educator, and while he was not out as a trans man in this job, he had recently come out as genderqueer.

When applying for this sex educator position, Sawyer was forced by his interviewer to "pick" a set of gender pronouns over the course of a stressful conversation. "[The interviewer] was like, 'you need to choose right now. You need to be comfortable so you need to tell me.' I was like, 'I just did tell you what I want, that I'm fine with either pronoun, it's not a big deal.' She's like, 'That's not an answer.' . . . So I just said 'she' because I thought that would secure the job for me."

While this interviewer spoke about the necessity of Sawyer working on LGBT training, his immediate supervisor forbade him from this type of work. "I couldn't even talk about it among the people outside of our team," Sawyer explained. For this reason, Sawyer is not yet out as trans at this workplace, though he recently came out as "genderqueer." What is most important to him is being able to look and act as authentically as possible—regardless of the identity labels he uses to do so.

Drew

Drew, a white transmasculine person in his twenties who uses he/him pronouns, had no interest in masculinizing HRT and has worked in the foodservice, retail, and medical industries while in the Bay Area.

Drew often experienced difficulties having his masculinity and his masculine identity validated. While working at an OB/GYN office, his best efforts to appear hypermasculine were unsuccessful in influencing his coworkers to use he/him pronouns. "It seemed like no matter how much I tried to exert my masculine side and be read as something rather than a girl, it didn't work." At his next job working for a hardware store, Drew insisted that others refer to him as "Drew" and with he/him pronouns, a request that many coworkers had difficulty honoring.

Drew then took up sales work at a clothing store, where his managers assigned him to the women's side of the store and his coworkers once again perceived him to be a woman. One coworker said, "I know that you are male but when I look at your face it just looks so round and feminine that I'm going to call you she." For Drew, the downsides of not undergoing HRT were being constantly perceived as either a woman or an adolescent boy. At the time of the interview, Drew believed this to be an acceptable consequence.

BUTCH WOMEN

Pat

Pat, a white butch woman in her fifties, uses she/her pronouns and identifies as a "tomboy." Pat has worked in the food service and shipping industries during her time in the Bay Area.

When Pat worked for a grocery store, her assertive communication style drove her to seek out more higher-paid positions. "I worked as a cashier two days . . . and I was promoted." Later, Pat lobbied aggressively for a raise. "I insisted on getting my pay raise and I fought for the pay raise. I fought. I went to the union. I went to the district manager . . . I wasn't afraid to say 'look, this is what's mine, I earned this.'"

If anything, Pat identified discrimination that other more feminine women received—in the form of catcalling, lowered wages, disrespect, and decreased authority—that she herself did not. Pat was unique among the people interviewed for not mentioning a single workplace discrimination experience.

Sam

Sam, a white and Latinx butch and genderqueer woman in their thirties who uses they/them pronouns, began presenting more masculine four years before the interview. In every work experience they discussed, they used she/her pronouns and were comfortable being perceived as a butch woman. Like Pat, Sam has faced little discrimination at work and spoke little of it over the course of their interview.

The discrimination Sam has faced has typically been during the interview process of hiring. In one story they shared, Sam's interviewer was clearly made uncomfortable by Sam's more masculine gender expression, and immediately dismissed them as a candidate. Overall, however, Sam's more masculine gender expression and interactional style have been a boon to them at work. At their job doing advertising and digital media work, Sam's direct and blunt communication style was well received by the other men in the workplace, and misogynistic bosses have overlooked Sam while discriminating against other women in the workplace.

Sam's aggressiveness was not always rewarded—occasionally, Sam would cross the line and be told to tone it down. In general, however, Sam was highly privileged in their workplace, and has faced next-to-no discrimination. "There's hiccups for sure but generally I'm given the same amount of prestige and respect as other cis[gender] men."

ASSIGNED FEMALE AT BIRTH NONBINARY/GENDERFLUID

Casey

Casey, an indigenous nonbinary person in their twenties who uses either he/him or they/them pronouns, had begun masculinizing HRT a year before their interview and has worked primarily as a veterinarian during their time in the Bay.

The first workplace where Casey was out as trans was at an animal clinic, where Casey mentioned their trans identity during their interview. "I let the hiring manager know during my interview I'm transgender and she said . . . 'I don't think that's something anybody needs to know.' " However, this same individual later outed Casey's trans identity to others in the office without their consent, which led to other employees there cornering Casey to ask invasive questions. As Casey continued to medically transition, the hiring manager began to more overtly discriminate against Casey by restricting their access to work opportunities. When a facilitated mediation between Casey and this manager failed, Casey decided to quit.

Casey made sure their next job, which was at a university animal clinic, was trans-friendly. The interviewer at this university position asked about Casey's preferred pronouns and validated their gender identity, showing them only the men's facilities at their request. The forwardness of this university in creating an inclusive environment was extremely valuable for Casey, and they were still working in this position at the time of the interview.

Hayden

Hayden, a white and Latinx nonbinary person in their twenties who uses they/them pronouns, began socially transitioning to a more masculine gender expression two years before the interview. Hayden stopped masculinizing HRT after six months after they became satisfied with their appearance.

One of the first experiences Hayden described concerned their employment at a restaurant they worked at as an assistant chef. Hayden's superiors at this place of employment often made backhanded comments undermining Hayden's masculinity, saying things like "You can't carry that pot, let a real man do it. You can't move that, let a real guy do it" and "Oh, you're lucky that you're in back of the house and not in the front of the house." Eventually, Hayden had enough and quit.

Since then, Hayden has worked part-time self-employed and making vegan sex toys, citing the lack of discrimination as a compelling motive to do this work. "I don't discriminate against myself," he quipped. To supplement their income, Hayden has also sought the assistance of the Trans Economic Empowerment Initiative, which has helped them apply for trans-friendly jobs. At the time of the interview, Hayden seemed excited by the prospects of future work.

Jordan

Jordan, a 56-year-old white agender person who uses no pronouns, has presented androgynously for more than thirty years. At the time of the interview, Jordan was working as a real estate agent.

While working as an electrician in the 1980s, Jordan described receiving intense discrimination in the form of verbal harassment and death threats. Jordan attributed this discrimination to being largely because Jordan was one of the only "women" in the union. After eight years as an electrician, Jordan began working as a realtor with an extremely uncooperative boss who took issue with Jordan's appearance. "She really hated me, the only thing I could think of was . . . that I was gay . . . or maybe it was how I presented because I wore men's suits. She really couldn't stand me," Jordan explains. After this job, Jordan worked as an insurance agent with another boss who criticized Jordan for not being "feminine enough." Jordan was still working at this job at the time of the interview, and seemed accustomed to the treatment received at this job.

Lee

Lee, a white "genderfluid" person in her thirties who is most frequently perceived by others to be a "bearded woman," uses she/her pronouns and began growing out her natural beard three years before the interview. Lee was working as a teacher at the time of the interview.

Lee often received street harassment in response to her gender-nonconforming appearance, with most comments directed at her beard. "I had one guy call me an abomination . . . I had one guy bellowing, 'That's disgusting, there's a bearded woman, that's disgusting.' " Despite this frequent harassment, however, Lee has received little discrimination in any of her employment experiences. While engaged in a teaching fellowship at a middle school, Lee was encouraged to talk about her beard with other teachers-in-training so as not to surprise them, but otherwise received no comments about her gender expression.

When she decided to continue growing out her beard, Lee briefed her students and her supervisors at the school. As she explained to them, "Well my beard just grows there. I just let it grow. Some women have beards, some guys don't. So I happen to have a beard." Aside from some brief questions, both students and supervisors accepted the explanation without protest, and Lee's employment experience has been otherwise uneventful.

Phoenix

Phoenix, a 28-year-old white nonbinary person who prefers the gender-neutral terms "this one or that one" as opposed to gender-neutral pronouns, was running a small business at the time of the interview.

In general, Phoenix faced little discrimination while living in the Bay Area due to the business that this one started doing catering and delivery. Much of this lack of discrimination may be attributed to Phoenix's lack of supervision, being self-employed, but Phoenix also noted that this one's business partner was not treated the same way by clients. "I am certainly offered more well-paying jobs more regularly than [my feminine presenting partner]. I think it's not just her presentation but also [differences in] our approach." While Phoenix is typically perceived to be a woman, Phoenix believed that this one's assertive interactional style and general gender expression have them advantages over feminine women, "I think that [feminine women] have a harder time getting away with being in control and being feminine . . . when they do it they sound more whiny. Our culture has taught me that."

Phoenix's attributed their lack of discrimination to their combination of a masculine interactional style with a more masculine gender expression. "I have a lot of privilege [because of] my voice and my speed, and the body that matches it."

ASSIGNED MALE AT BIRTH NONBINARY/GENDERFLUID

Cameron

Cameron, a 40-year-old white genderfluid person who uses a mixture of he/him and she/her pronouns depending on how masculine or feminine Cameron is feeling in a given moment, has no interest in HRT and was working at a temp agency at the time of the interview.

After graduating from College, Cameron went to a job fair for trans people wearing feminine clothing, but felt uneasy in response to the subtle discomfort many of the recruiters seemed to show. At another job fair, one recruiter asked, "If I get you this cattle call job, can you present consistently over the course of assignment?" Though Cameron abided by these instructions and dressed consistently over that week, Cameron was never called back by the temp agency.

Cameron eventually decided to stop mentioning gender fluidity to get a job, and was able to be hired once this happened. At the time of the interview, Cameron was contemplating raising the topic of gender fluidity now that financial needs have been temporarily met. When she asked her boss at the temp agency she currently works for, Cameron's boss has disallowed her from arriving at work with a more feminine gender expression. "Her stated concern," Cameron explained, "was about consistency of presentation and the way she phrased it was concern for other people in the office being distracted." Cameron took this news with some disappointment, but wasn't willing to push the issue. "I'm incredibly reluctant to lose this job," Cameron explained.

Cory

Cory, a white nonbinary person in their twenties who has taken feminizing HRT on and off for seven years before the interview, has worked mostly in the foodservice industry during their time in the Bay Area.

Before moving to California, Cory was fired for their gender expression while working at cafes on the East Coast. At the first, their manager had been getting complaints about "a man with boobs working behind the counter," and quietly reduced Cory's hours until they had to leave. At another cafe, Cory reported the harassment they faced from a coworker to the owners, who accused Cory of trying to take this coworker's job and fired Cory instead.

Cory has worked in a restaurant for most of their time since moving to California. Upon working there, Cory began taking significant effort to pass as a cisgender woman, beginning to dress with a "hyper-femininity that I tactically employ for food service work." Initially, Cory was still viewed as a man. "All of the Spanish speaking kitchen called me amigo and it really hurt my feelings. I'm like, 'Guys, why are you saying that? I'm a girl. Call me amiga.' " Others at this workplace frequently brought up Cory's trans status at work. "One of the delivery guys at work came and was like, 'Do you ever dance at [a trans nightclub]?' " Another coworker makes a point of demonstrating that Cory isn't a "real" woman by explicitly telling them whenever she is on her period. "She made a point of saying wherever she was bleeding. She'd be like, 'I'm going to go be a girl now' [as if to say] 'you can never touch the fact that your ovaries will never bleed.' "

Jessie

Jessie, a Latinx nonbinary person in their forties who uses they/them pronouns, began socially and medically transitioning to a more feminine gender expression 13 years before the interview but had recently begun moving back toward androgyny.

During the first decade of their transition when Jessie identified as a trans woman, they received significant hiring discrimination in response to the lower pitch of their voice, receiving numerous rejections from jobs they were extremely overqualified for. Eventually, Jessie found a job working for a Spanish-language newspaper, but then encountered pervasive misgendering at work. Jessie's complaints to HR yielded only half-hearted attempts to change coworkers' behaviors, and Jessie decided to take matters into their own hands and began asking their coworkers to use the pronouns they preferred at the time, she/her. Almost immediately, Jessie's supervisors began taking efforts to push Jessie out of the workplace. "They tried to like pile as many things on me as possible just to see if I could just bear with it, handle it or what not. But there were obviously just looking for any excuse they could think of [to fire me]." This experience contributed to Jessie's decision to leave the field of journalism.

Jessie began to avoid jobs in which face-to-face interaction was necessary. "It became so traumatic for me to deal with [discrimination] and I was just so scared . . . that I would get a job and that somehow something I would do would get me in trouble and either get me fired." Jessie began freelance writing in their own time, a compromise that allowed them to avoid discrimination by picking clients carefully.

"Occasionally if you have a client that you don't think that things are going too great [with] . . . you can just end the relationship," they elaborated.

Rory

Rory, a Latinx intersex and nonbinary person in their twenties who uses they/them pronouns, had been on feminizing HRT three years before the interview but stopped for personal reasons.

Rory's gender expression has often been the target of teasing and harassment. While working as a phone bank, Rory faced extremely invasive questions directed at their trans history and their genitalia. At a mechanic shop, coworkers would ask mocking questions like, "Don't you think it's about time you stopped taking hormones?" As a community organizer, they were asked to hide their trans identity and try to pass as either a cisgender man or woman when talking with immigrants. At a more recent job working at a school, Rory had their clothing choices micromanaged and policed, and their principal ordered them not to "confuse the kids." The only gender-neutral bathroom in this school was often locked, and Rory would often choose not to use the bathroom rather than ask for the key.

The best work environment for Rory, given all this, was self-employment. "It doesn't matter that I'm trans, it doesn't matter that I present in any way," Rory explained. "I could be doing the work in a skirt or I could be doing the work naked." Having the freedom to express themselves authentically was invaluable for Rory.

Rowan

Rowan, a white nonbinary person in their twenties who uses they/them pronouns, began requesting gender-neutral pronouns two years before the interview. At the time of the interview, Rowan was working in the tech industry.

Rowan, while working for a mobile app company, began experimenting with their gender expression by coming to work some days dressed more feminine and other days dressed more masculine. Rowan immediately noticed that their work was scrutinized more closely and evaluated more critically on their more feminine days. An HR representative began to heavily police their clothing, with Rowan stating that "she was concerned about how I presented would impact other people's perception of the company." When Rowan mentioned the discrimination they were facing from this representative to their boss, they received a lackluster, noncommittal response. This lack of support, coupled with the ongoing harassment they received from the HR representative, prompted them to quit.

Their next job at a tech company was more trans-friendly, and Rowan's immediate team was far more supportive than coworkers at their last job. Rowan spoke, however, of an incident where an employee confronted them in the bathroom, saying, "You are in the wrong place. You need to leave." While this was the only discrimination experience from their new workplace Rowan commented on, it clearly impacted them. Rowan admitted that they did not report this discrimination, seeming hopeful that it wouldn't happen again.

CHAPTER THREE

The Anatomy of Discrimination

Research on trans discrimination is not new. In the late 1990s, Patricia Gagné, Richard Tewksbury, and Deanna McGaughey reported on the experiences of trans women and genderqueer employees in the labor market. They found that individuals who changed their gender expression on the job experienced rejection and harassment from coworkers and were often demoted, pressured to quit, or fired, with only a few maintaining their jobs (Gagné, Tewksbury, McGaughey 1997; Gagné and Tewksbury 1998). As a result, many became under-employed; accepted jobs that offered less pay, security, and prestige; or remained unemployed after transitioning. Trans people who tried to maintain their same job during their transition experienced substantial pressure to transition quickly and convincingly. Their contact with the public was limited until—and only if—they could pass convincingly as a "normal" man or woman (Gagné and Tewksbury 1998).

More recently, research into trans employment discrimination in the San Francisco Bay Area revealed that these disparities continue, even in a region championed as the "most LGBT-inclusive in the world." A 2006 study reported that 35 percent of the trans people surveyed were unemployed, and of those employed, 57 percent reported employment discrimination, 40 percent reported discrimination in hiring, 19 percent reported discrimination in promotion opportunities, and 18 percent reported being fired due to their gender identity. Almost 25 percent reported sexual harassment and 21 percent reported verbal harassment at work. Although California amended an antidiscrimination law called the Fair Employment and Housing Act to include trans individuals in 2004, only 12 percent indicated that they filed any kind of complaint for the discrimination they experienced (Transgender Law Center 2006). Even in 2008, four years after trans people were granted statewide legal protection, 70 percent of the trans individuals surveyed reported experiencing harassment or discrimination in their workplace (Transgender Law Center 2009). The survey indicates that 22 percent of respondents were harassed by coworkers, 17 percent were harassed by their supervisors, 15 percent were sexually harassed, 9 percent had their access to customers or clients restricted or eliminated, 22 percent felt they were unfairly scrutinized or disciplined, 13 percent were denied a promotion, 14 percent were fired, 12 percent were laid off, and 10 percent were reorganized out of a job. Despite being protected under the law, only 15 percent of the respondents who experienced harassment or discrimination filed a complaint of any kind and only 31 percent of the complaints filed were resolved favorably.

Surveys taken outside of the San Francisco Bay Area reveal similar findings across the United States. In 2011, the National Center for Transgender Equality and the National Gay and Lesbian Task Force published a report outlining the most extensive national transgender discrimination survey conducted to date (Grant et al. 2011). The study found that respondents experienced unemployment at twice the national rate, while trans people of color experienced unemployment up to four times that rate. Harassment was nearly universal, as 90 percent reported experienced harassment or mistreatment or took actions to avoid it while working. About half of respondents reported experiencing underemployment, being fired, not hired, or denied a promotion because of their trans identity or gender expression. Many tried to avoid discrimination, with 71 percent hiding their gender identity or transition and 57 percent delaying transitioning. Trans people of color experienced discrimination at two to three times this rate. Nonbinary respondents, who indicated a variety of identities including genderqueer, pangender, third gender, and Two-Spirit, were slightly less likely to lose their job due to bias (19 percent compared to 27 percent) but are more likely to be out of work (76 percent as compared to 56 percent) and were slightly more likely to work in the underground economy (20 percent as compared to 15 percent) (Harrison, Grant, and Herman 2012). In the U.S. trans survey, a follow-up study conducted in 2015, 15 percent of respondents who had a job in the past year experienced verbal, physical, and/or sexual harassment at work; 30 percent were fired, denied a promotion, or experienced some other form of mistreatment; and 77 percent took steps to avoid mistreatment in the workplace, including hiding or delaying their transition and quitting (James et al. 2016).

DISCRIMINATION'S MANY FACES

The stories that follow briefly summarize the experiences of the gender-diverse people interviewed, and reveal similar rates of discrimination as the research mentioned above.

Hiring, Unemployment, and Settling for Less

Of our respondents, more than half experienced discrimination in hiring, and many remarked on instances of discriminatory practices, profiling, and bias within the hiring process. Kai, a white transmasculine person in his thirties, shared stories of having job offers rescinded after employers examined his driver's license. Jessie and Alex spoke about the difficulties caused by the pitch of their voices during interviews. Sam, Whitney, and Cameron spoke to the many different reactions interviewers give to trans applicants, and how all of them nonetheless resulted in not being hired.

Of those interviewees who were unemployed at the time of the interview, all were trans women. Alex, Whitney, and Kelly were highly qualified in their respective fields before transitioning, but have been unable to secure a job since transition. Kelly, a white trans woman in her sixties, stated matter-of-factly, "people don't hire transsexuals [sic] . . . if [employers] got a choice, why take the queer when you got a perfectly good something else?" While only these three were unemployed, the threat of unemployment hung over nearly all of the people interviewed, even those who were able to find a job.

This threat of unemployment often forces individuals to lower their standards and settle for less, prioritizing any employment over unemployment. Despite her teaching experience, Taylor, a white trans woman in her thirties, ended up working at an entry-level position at an LGBT hotel. Robin, a white trans woman in her fifties, did not leave her union even after receiving massive cuts to her pay and work opportunities after transitioning. Kai, even while being under-employed and exploited by employers in Arizona who knew about their hiring difficulties, stayed in the same position. Many of these individuals had to put aside their own pride and dignity, choosing to accept unskilled, degrading, or discriminatory jobs because it was uncertain whether after leaving they could be hired anywhere else.

Discrimination on the Job

Discrimination in the workplace was a universal reality for all of the gender-diverse people in this book, with every interviewee able to speak about at least one experience during their work histories that felt discriminatory. In the stories they told, discrimination took many forms. Many participants spoke about being misgendered—referred to by the wrong gender and pronouns—by colleagues or supervisors. Some spoke about being outed: having their trans status or transition history revealed to others without their consent. Others talked about verbal harassment, whether in the form of invasive questioning, religious proselytizing, or insults and derogatory comments. Still others discussed more subtle experiences of discrimination like exclusion from gendered spaces, loss of respect, increased scrutiny, and micromanaging.

Many gender-diverse people experienced micromanaging once their gender expression began to change. Rowan, a white nonbinary person in their twenties, described how the respect they received dropped after varying their gender expression at their mobile app company, and how they were more likely to be micromanaged on days they were presenting more feminine at work. Leslie, a white trans woman in her thirties, described how after transitioning she became a token at her biotech company and felt like others were "looking for slip-ups" from her. Robin, a white trans woman in her fifties, found that she wasn't taken as seriously at her union workplace after transitioning. "I wound up spending a lot more time explaining what I am doing and why than I ever did before." Rory, a Latinx nonbinary person in their twenties, felt like they were micromanaged at a school they worked at due to their ambiguous gender expression and explained that their boss "would make me do the same job twice or they would have someone else check it." All but one of the interviewees who experienced micromanaging in the workplace ended up leaving their place of employment due to feelings of heightened stress and discomfort.

Exclusion from gendered spaces is often a result of transition, especially for nonbinary or genderfluid people. Sawyer and Rowan both discussed the discomfort they feel when surrounded by only cisgender women or cisgender men, as if they belonged to neither group. Parker, a white trans man in his twenties, discussed this feeling of exclusion succinctly in his job as a sales analyst, saying, "There was this kind of men's space here and women's space here, I just wasn't necessarily welcome more or less to either place. So I would kind of sit somewhere in the middle ... so it was just kind of secret social space, I wasn't really allowed to bridge either."

One of the most pervasive experiences, however, was misgendering at work. Cory's kitchen staff coworkers misgendered them and justified it by arguing that Cory, a white nonbinary person in their twenties, had "masculine energy." Drew, a white transmasculine person in his twenties, asked explicitly for he/him pronouns while working at an OB/GYN office and was told, "Sorry we're not going to bother with that." Taylor, a white trans woman in her thirties, described the impact of misgendering when she explained that " 'him,' 'she-him,' 'sir,' that bothers me worse than 'fuck you bitch, tranny whore' or whatever. Pronoun usage, wrong pronoun usage is much more hurtful to me than curse words." For genderqueer, genderfluid, or otherwise nonbinary-identifying interviewees, this misgendering was a frequent occurrence. Cory was shouted at by an administrator at a coffee shop, "We're not going to call you [by the gender-neutral pronouns] ze and hir—it's an either or world!" Kai, a white transmasculine person in his thirties, was called a "pretend man" by his boss in his current job as a veterinary technician.

For those gender-diverse people who suppress their trans identity at work, or are more selective about letting others know, the threat of being outed in the workplace is a real one. Casey, an indigenous non-binary person in their twenties, had a manager at the first animal clinic they worked at who outed their trans status to coworkers during a staff meeting, opening Casey up to future harassment. Leslie's co-worker shouted her former name down a hallway within earshot of many people who did not know of Leslie's transition.

Half of our interviewees faced invasive questioning in their work-places, and explicitly spoke about the discomfort and unhappiness associated with responding to it. After Casey was outed, they were cornered by a coworker at a time when they were unprepared to edu-cate. "I usually try to answer those [questions] but at that point I had just broken up with a long-term partner and I started crying and it was really uncomfortable." Leslie, a white trans woman in her thirties, found herself educating a coworker who "came off as very insincere and put me on my guard" who asked invasive questions about her plan for surgery. Cory, a white nonbinary person in their twenties, had multiple experiences at the restaurant they work in which coworkers would engage them in trans-related conversations. As Cory put a significant effort into passing, these uninitiated conversations felt invasive and delegitimizing. "One of the delivery guys at work came and was like, 'Do you ever dance at [a trans nightclub]?' Like I'm not fucking out to them. I show up to work trying get people to call me in the binary—just dude, you deliver our lettuce. Where the fuck do you get off asking me if I dance at [that nightclub]? Rory, a Latinx nonbinary person in their twenties, was often directed invasive ques-tions about their body and transition history due to their ambiguous gender expression. At a phone bank, a colleague asked, "What are you?"

Perhaps the most prevalent harassment came in the form of gender policing as coworkers would often exert pressure for participants to adopt a gender expression more in line with conventional gender norms. Cameron, a 40-year-old white genderfluid person, was told to compromise their genderfluid expression in exchange for a job at a temp agency. The hiring manager asked them, "If I get you this cattle call job . . . can you present consistently over the course of assignment?" Cassidy, an Asian American transmasculine person in their twenties, had a boss at their law office who told them they sounded like a "valley girl," and that, as a result, they would not be allowed to take phone calls from clients. "It's a whole attitude that people just want you to like man up really quickly. If you're a man this is the way a man is." Rowan, a white nonbinary person in their twenties, was heavily policed by their boss's wife and an HR representative while working at a mobile app company, and was told explicitly, "Don't wear a dress, don't wear makeup."

Rory, a Latinx nonbinary person in their twenties, experienced perhaps the highest amount of this kind of discrimination. While organizing for immigrant rights, they were told, "Could you not present yourself as trans when you're speaking to these immigrant people?" When working as a volunteer substitute teacher, they were reprimanded for their gender-nonconforming appearance and told that they should "set the example . . . and shouldn't confuse the kids."

More explicit verbal harassment occurred as well. At the bike shop where Rory worked, coworkers would mockingly ask them, "Don't you think it's about time you stopped taking hormones?" At the hospital facility, Taylor, a white trans woman in her thirties, received intense harassment from the youth she counseled. "There was a lot of, 'Fucking man chick, you look like a fucking dude!'" Kai, while working in a veterinary clinic, was told, "You should go to church. Maybe that would heal you." Cassidy, an Asian American transmasculine person in their twenties, while working as a microbiologist, had coworkers who were "always questioning, just looking at me like I was I guess like this freakish person or some sort of a deviant." While working as a stagehand, Robin was told, "Do you think you are going to get into heaven looking like that? I mean, what are you? Some kind of crossdresser? You know you're going to burn in hell."

Sometimes this verbal harassment was accompanied with sexual harassment. While these experiences were rare, those who experienced it described the intense discomfort and stress these instances caused. During a Bring-Your-Child-to-Work day at the tech company they worked in, Rowan, a white nonbinary person in their twenties, overheard two children of other employees discussing Rowan's gender. They tried to resolve their debate by looking under the table, presumably to check for Rowan's genitalia under their kilt. Blake, a mixed trans man in his twenties, described how in his shipment job he had a coworker remark that it was "really sad that the most masculine person here doesn't have a penis." Cory, a white nonbinary person in their twenties, had a coworker in the restaurant they worked in who openly discussed her menstrual cycle to emphasize that because Cory did not experience periods they could not be a woman. "She made a point of saying wherever she was bleeding. She'd be like, 'I'm going to go be a girl now' [as if to say] you can never touch the fact that your ovaries will never bleed."

Three of the interviewees experienced physical threats to their well-being. While in Arizona, Kai, a white transmasculine person in his thirties, had "six guys headed towards me yelling, taunting. It was horrible . . . [They] pretty much chased me to my truck. They were calling faggot, lesbian." Jordan, a 56-year-old white agender person, while working as an electrician, received "murder and rape threats all the time. Mostly murder threats."

Many of the interviewees shared tense stories about bathrooms and the stress, anxiety, and fear accompanied with seeking them out. While teaching at a middle school, Lee, a white "genderfluid" person in her thirties, made the trek to remote bathrooms to avoid conflict. Parker, before transitioning at work, tried to avoid using work bathrooms altogether. Rowan and Rory were confronted in both men's and women's bathrooms, leaving them no remaining facilities to use. Rowan, a white nonbinary person in their twenties, explained that "being asked to leave the men's restroom was also kind of uncomfortable . . . [yet] I feel some stress when I go to use the women's washroom, I don't know what is going to happen."

Rory, a Latinx nonbinary person in their twenties, once was escorted out of both the women's and men's restrooms. "I went into the men's restroom and the security guard was actually brought into the restroom and escorted me out of the restroom. He says, 'Excuse me ma'am but I'm going to have to escort you out of the restroom for your safety.' I was done so I [said] 'Well all right, fine. Whatever.' I left . . . this happened Monday and then Wednesday again I'm at the same bus station and I use the women's restroom wearing the same clothes. The *same* security guard is brought into the restroom this time by a woman who was fearing for her safety . . . the security guard is at the door saying, 'Excuse me sir I'm going to have to escort you out of the restroom for this woman's safety.' Right. It takes the attendant a little while to kind of register what happens. They see my face and they see that I'm wearing the same clothes and they're like, 'Wait a minute are you the same person from a couple of days ago?' I'm like, 'Yes, that's me.' He's like, 'Well, okay. I'm escorting you from both restrooms now.'"

Leaving the Workplace

Many of the gender-diverse people interviewed told stories of leaving a workplace, and almost every instance mentioned was related to discrimination.

Some were fired due to their trans identity. Cory, a white nonbinary person in their twenties, shared that while working in a Boston cafe, "the owner of the café had the manager take me off the schedule and it was shared with me through a roundabout way that he had been getting complaints about a man with boobs working behind the counter. And then I was discreetly shuffled off the schedule and there was no more work for me. So there was never a 'we're firing you because you're trans [moment],' but it was made clear to me that I was not working there anymore because I was trans."

Additionally, many of the people interviewed described experiences in which they were fired after varying their gender expression or transitioning at work, but were not able to concretely link their termination to their changing gender expression. For example, Whitney, a white trans woman in her twenties, was fired from her machine shop a week after beginning HRT, after several months of comments about her feminine gender expression.

When not explicitly fired for being trans, many of the gender-diverse people interviewed described being pressured to leave. In most of these cases, employers attempted to create a workplace environment so hostile—whether through policies, verbal harassment, or exclusion—that gender-diverse employees had no choice but to quit. Casey, an indigenous nonbinary person in their twenties, had a manager at an animal clinic who outed them to the rest of the staff and attempted to sabotage their career. "She was not allowing me to do anything to help me gain experience [and forbade other employees to train me]. In order to become a technician at that clinic, you had to complete a checklist of all these tasks and have a supervisor sign off on a checklist. And she wasn't letting me do anything ... she didn't want me to be allowed to do anything except clean and stock." When this manager's behavior escalated after Casey set up a mediated conversation, they knew it was time to go. "It was just so stressful that I was like I need to get out of there."

Jessie, a Latinx nonbinary person in their forties, asked for coworkers at the Spanish newspaper they worked at to use "she/her" pronouns but had those requests ignored, both by coworkers and by the HR department. Jessie began correcting people herself, saying "It was not too long after I started like trying to correct people about pronouns that they actually started making things very, very uncomfortable for me . . . they no longer really felt comfortable with my being there . . . I would say that they tried to like pile as many things on me as possible just to see if I could just bear with it, handle it or what not. But there were obviously just looking for any excuse they could think of."

Kai's story is perhaps the most dramatic. While working as an ophthalmologist in Arizona, Kai, a white transmasculine person in his thirties, informed his boss that he would be transitioning and undergoing HRT. While initially receptive, once Kai's gender expression began to change, Kai's boss didn't follow through. "He treated me like a piece of shit. I went from being his right-hand technician . . . I was his fill-in-the-blank person. I was his surgical gofer. After [transitioning], I was a piece of shit to him. I was less than a kennel attendant. I was not even good enough to clean up shit." Kai's boss put Kai on an unsustainable work schedule and slashed his pay. Kai tried going to HR, but when his representative made a fuss on Kai's behalf, Kai's boss had the representative replaced. This act made it clear that Kai would not receive any protection from discrimination, and Kai had no choice but to quit.

The high salience of these stories of discrimination—and the severity of the consequences for the people featured in them—are not lost on members of gender-diverse communities. Many of the interviewees we spoke to who considered transitioning at work or changing their gender expression in some way mentioned their fear of discrimination as a primary reason why they chose to quit preemptively or avoid employment while transitioning.

Alex, a white trans woman in her forties, quit her job as an executive at a tech company after watching another trans colleague's career stagnate after coming out at work. After Alex quit, however, she began to regret her choice. At the time of the interview, though Alex acknowledged that staying "would have been a risk," she wished that she "had stayed and at least tried to figure it out in retrospect." Jessie, a Latinx nonbinary person in their forties, had to give up what they felt could have been a promising career in journalism after their transition. They explained, "it's no longer possible, at least not in my opinion, to become a globetrotting journalist and go through all these dangerous parts of the world where even here in the Bay Area there's people getting killed for being trans or non-conforming."

Cassidy, who worked for many years as a microbiologist, chose to leave that job and avoid employment altogether during their transition out of this fear. "I do not want people to see me during this transitional time. I don't want to face any discrimination, I don't want to have any problems."

Many of those who leave the workplace, whether voluntarily or involuntarily, eventually find themselves needing to rejoin it. Some must do so eventually out of financial need, while others wait to complete a social and/or medical transition. Regardless, gender-diverse people at this end of the cycle find themselves back at its beginning, navigating the many obstacles associated with hiring. Many find, as the cycle repeats itself, that they will face hiring discrimination, fears of unemployment, and the realities of settling for less. In their jobs, many will experience discrimination on the job, whether in the form of harassment, exclusion, higher standards, or violence that pressures them to leave.

Even in the San Francisco Bay Area, the strain of living in this vicious cycle was glaring.

THE LUCKY FEW

Many of these experiences highlighted the extent of the vicious cycle of discrimination. While we expected to find cases in which gender-diverse people were able to mitigate or avoid discrimination in some ways, for most of our interviewees this was by no means an easy feat. If discrimination could be avoided, it was often only temporarily, partially, or undertaken at a huge personal cost. But not so for some interviewees: five of our interviewees reported little to no discrimination over the entirety of their workplace histories despite being gender-diverse.

Leslie, a white trans woman in her thirties, transitioned on the job at a biotech company and was the only trans woman interviewed who spoke positively about the workplace she transitioned in. HR played a huge role in Leslie's experiences: her HR department sent out a company-wide email with information about nondiscrimination policy and coordinated a long weekend for Leslie to leave work during which a renowned trans advocate was flown in to train her coworkers. Leslie explains, "I don't feel like I've lost a huge degree of male privilege," and is the only trans woman we interviewed who expressed this sentiment after transitioning. Leslie attributes this experience to her industry. "I work with scientists, with people who are degreed, etcetera. I'm not trying to be like ivory tower here, but it's like there is a different mindset than you would find at McDonalds or in a factory or something like that." It is worth noting that many other gender-diverse interviewees working in similar industries experienced heavier discrimination, which suggests to us that other factors contributed to Leslie's positive experience.

Parker, a white trans man in his twenties, experienced the bulk of his discrimination experiences when he was perceived as a butch woman in his sales analyst position. When Parker chose to come out in his workplace as a trans man, he himself was surprised by how amenable his colleagues were. "Most of the men in my office—not once did any one slip up with names. Never has anyone screwed up pronouns or anything. I didn't expect that—I kind of figured it would kind of be half-and-half for a while but it never happened." Parker remarks that after transitioning, he felt "instantly in the boys club" and that this was accompanied with improvements to the way he was treated, the authority he was given, and the respect he received from others, all developments that Parker in large part was not expecting. "I was shocked at how instantly, especially with male colleagues, the hurdles of being a [butch] woman in the workplace fell down." There was only one catch—Parker's newfound status in the boy's club weakened their relationship with women coworkers with whom he had once been close. "It made them really uncomfortable that I knew these things about them, these personal things about them."

Pat, a white butch woman in her fifties, has very rarely faced discrimination over the span of her work history. When she did, she voluntarily removed herself from discriminatory situations by requesting job changes or directly resolving conflicts with disagreeable coworkers. In all of her workplaces, Pat's confidence and assertiveness helped her succeed, and Pat herself identifies instances where she was treated better than more feminine cisgender women.

Phoenix, a 28-year-old white nonbinary person, also largely avoided discrimination. Phoenix attributed this lack of discrimination to being self-employed and an assertive interactional style coupled with a more masculine gender expression. "I answer quickly and I answer loudly, so people want that . . . I think I have a lot of privilege [because of] my voice and my speed, and the body that matches it." Phoenix is acutely aware of the experiences faced by the more feminine business partner in the small business the two run. "I think that [feminine women] have a harder time getting away with being in control and being feminine . . . when they do it they sound more whiny. Our culture has taught me that."

Lee, a white "genderfluid" person in her thirties, has faced little workplace discrimination despite being seen by many as a "bearded woman." Lee's lack of workplace discrimination stems primarily from her comfort with modifying her gender expression—shaving her beard, in particular—to be seen as acceptable during the interview process. But when Lee chose to grow her beard back out while working at a religious private school, she was still able to avoid discrimination. To her bosses, she explained, " 'I'm going to grow my beard back out. I've done this before and it wasn't a problem so that's what I'm doing, just so you know, and it doesn't mean I'm transitioning or changing anything else. I'm just growing my beard.' They were like, 'okay.' " To the students she taught, she simply explained that "some women have beards, some guys don't. So I happen to have a beard." Lee faced no discrimination in this environment.

FILLING IN THE BLANKS

In this chapter, we documented and categorized the types of discrimination our interviewees experienced, from anti-trans hiring bias to misgendering to verbal abuse. We took special note of those who spoke about facing little or no discrimination, and established that these stories were the exception, not the rule. Our conclusion would be that gender-diverse people face a wide range of discrimination at all stages of employment, and that the repercussions for deviating from society's normative ideas of gender identity and expression can be severe. At the same time, discrimination is not inevitable: many interviewees described times when they expected to face discrimination but didn't, and some interviewees hardly faced any discrimination at all.

In later chapters, we dive deeply into the stories of the 25 gender-diverse interviewees to hunt for patterns and insights that any one story alone cannot give. The clues from this detective work come from the folk explanations that the interviewees provide, the observations we as social scientists pull out from multiple interviewees, and finally knowledge from the academic fields of social psychology, sociology, gender studies, and queer theory. We put forward the explanations we do with the knowledge that these are hypotheses and educated guesses at best. They cannot and should not be replacements for more research and examination, but in an ideal world can give future social scientists a place to begin. And for gender-diverse communities in the Bay Area and beyond, they may play the important role of validating and making sense of discrimination that at times can feel overwhelming and incomprehensible.

To end this chapter, we will ask a series of questions that emerge from the stories above.

- What are the factors that contribute to a discriminatory action occurring to a trans person, in general?

- What similarities, if any, exist among the discrimination experiences of people who identify similarly—trans men/transmasculine people, trans women/transfeminine people, butch women, and nonbinary people? Why?
- How do the experiences of our interviewees support or challenge existing research on gender discrimination in the workplace?
- What differences exist, if any, between the experiences of binary-identifying gender-diverse people and nonbinary-identifying gender-diverse people?

CHAPTER FOUR

On Men, Women, and Hegemony

The field of sociology is already teeming with research literature on gender, though the wealth of existing literature has looked predominantly at cisgender men and women. Whether our study of transgender men and women (and transmasculine and transfeminine people) proves an interesting riff on existing knowledge or perhaps challenges existing knowledge altogether, it is useful to at least present a quick overview of the literature.

CISGENDER STATUS INEQUALITY AND WORKPLACE DISCRIMINATION

Even before a child's birth, Western society socializes humans as one of two discrete, different genders. Boys are taught to be strong, take risks, and be dominant and physical; girls are taught to be timid, cautious, submissive, and emotional. As these behaviors are continually performed, they are assumed to be essential gender differences that justify the inequalities they produce in the workplace and other gendered environments (Fenstermaker, West, and Zimmerman 2002; West and Zimmerman 1987). In this way, the idea that masculinity is of higher status and higher value than femininity is one that both creates and relies on societal gender inequities (Connell 1987; Schippers 2007).

Not all masculinity is the same, however. Just as there are many types of men in the world, so too are there many kinds of masculinity—or "ways to be a man." At the top of all these is *hegemonic masculinity,* a conceptualization of the dominant form(s) of masculinity privileged over other subordinate or alternate masculinities—and femininities as well.

These dominant masculinities are not fixed and unchanging fortresses; rather, hegemonic masculinity evolves over time, taking bits and pieces from other kinds of masculinity to stay on top. A modern-day example: as the visibility of gay men has increased, one might argue that hegemonic masculinity has cherry-picked a stereotypical trait of this subordinate masculinity (say, fashion sense) and evolved accordingly. Thus, the dominant masculinity of today may very well be more well dressed and fashionable than the dominant masculinity several decades before (Connell and Messerschmidt 2005; Demetriou 2001).

Hegemonic masculinity is everywhere. It shows up visibly in social media, in advertisements, and in the lead actors of movies. It shows up less visibly—but perhaps more insidiously—as the intangible standard that people everywhere prize as the "ideal" or "most attractive" or "optimal" masculinity. The far-reaching nature of hegemonic masculinity in society severely restricts the range of acceptable alternative masculinities as a means of creating and assigning a status hierarchy. Men who adequately meet the expectations of hegemonic masculinity—and there are perhaps, by definition, few—occupy the highest level of gender status in society. Men who do not sufficiently perform hegemonic masculinity, including effeminate men, gay men, trans men, and genderqueer people, often face stigma and ridicule (Willer et al. 2013). This public enforcement of hegemonic masculinity functions at least partially as a means by which men can prove their heterosexuality and masculinity to other men: by ridiculing and mocking those who embody subordinate masculinities, others can situate themselves on the side of hegemonic masculinities (Franklin 2000; Kimmel 1994).

During childhood and teenage years, this ridicule often takes the form of teasing and bullying. During the adult stage, this ridicule often takes the form of prejudice and discrimination. The relentless teasing "sissy boys" receive (Rivers 2001), the popular "fag discourse" among adolescents (Pascoe 2005), and the consistency of which men who are perceived to be weak are told to "man up" are all ways in which gender stereotypes function to preserve gender differences that legitimize the status hierarchy. Over time, and on a large scale, this ridicule serves both as a method of asserting dominance and as a form of pressure intended to socialize men into a more socially validated masculine gender expression.

Hegemonic masculinity doesn't only affect men; women, too, are prescribed roles and expectations under the gender hierarchy. Women are low status and are expected to be communal, meaning that they ought to be interdependent, agreeable, nurturing, and modest. Men are high status and are expected to be agentic, meaning that they should be independent, assertive, ambitious, and self-promoting (Deaux and Kite 1993; Eagly 1987; Moss-Racusin et al. 2010; Williams and Best 1982). Thus, femininity is associated with communal behavior and masculinity is associated with agentic behavior. When women act in an agentic manner or when men act communal, they are often subject to social and economic backlash as a result of perceived status violations. These social sanctions can take the form of interpersonal punishment, including teasing, social exclusion, and harassment, or structural penalizations like denial of opportunities, restriction of privileges, and other forms of discrimination. According to the status incongruity hypothesis, one motivation for such backlash is that it helps maintain the status quo of the gender hierarchy (Rudman et al. 2012). In other words, men and women are told by the gender hierarchy that each should "know their place."

The backlash effect has been observed for a variety of counter-stereotypic gendered behaviors. Men who choose to stay home to take care of their children are disliked and perceived as low status (Brescoll and Uhlmann 2005). Men who choose to self-disclose their problems to a stranger are viewed as more psychologically disturbed than women who engage in the same behavior (Derlega and Chaiken 1976). Women leaders are more negatively evaluated when they display a directive rather than participatory style (Eagly, Makhijani, and Klonsky 1992). When speaking publicly, women are more persuasive when their style is orientated toward people rather than tasks (Carli, LaFleur, and Loeber 1995). Generally, competent women are viewed as cold (Wiley and Eskilon 1985) and undesirable members of a group (Hagen and Kahn 1975).

How does this play out in the workplace? One ramification of the status hierarchy is that employers evaluate men and women differently (Acker 1990; Kanter 1977; Williams 1992; Yoder 1994; Padavic and Reskin 2002), and counter-stereotypic gendered behaviors in the labor market trigger significant consequences. Communal men are believed to be less competent and hirable (Rudman 1998; Rudman and Glick 1999). Modest men have been shown to suffer hiring discrimination as modesty is seen as a violation of masculinity (Moss-Racusin et al. 2010). Although agentic women are viewed as qualified for leadership positions, they are discriminated against in hiring and face various forms of prejudice (Rudman 1998; Rudman and Glick 1999, 2001), including often being bypassed for promotions (Heilman 2001; Lyness and Judiesch 1999). Although women earn more when they work in predominantly male occupations, they are still paid less than men (England 1992). When identical, women's resumes are more negatively evaluated than those of men (Olian, Schwab, and Haberfeld 1988). In typically masculine jobs, successful women are not rated as likable as successful men, which can negatively affect their performance evaluations (Eagly, Makhijani, and

Klonsky 1992; Yoder 1994) and salary recommendations (Heilman et al. 2004).

Men are rewarded in a linear fashion; the more masculine men are, the better. Women, however, face a much more complicated equation for achieving success. Women receive a backlash for acting agentic and being assertive (Phelan, Moss-Racusin, and Rudman 2008; Rudman 1998; Rudman and Glick 1999, 2001), but only those who act agentic are deemed competent. Thus, women face a double bind in which they aren't able to show their competency without being perceived as agentic and nonfeminine and are thus penalized regardless (Eagly and Carli 2007; Eagly and Karau 2002). In order for women in the workplace to be perceived as competent, able workers and simultaneously avoid backlash for being unfeminine, they must precariously find the balance of displaying their competency and skills in a cooperative and group-oriented manner.

TRANS STATUS INEQUALITY AND DISCRIMINATION IN THE WORKPLACE

When we ask what factors go into the discrimination experiences of a "trans woman" or "trans man," it is important to attempt to disambiguate discrimination happening because of "trans," discrimination happening because of "woman/man," and discrimination happening because of "trans woman/trans man." That is to say, we must assume that binary-identifying trans people must deal with additional discrimination based on their trans status *in addition* to discrimination faced by people of their gender. Trans women will thus share some discrimination experiences in common with trans men (trans status discrimination) and cisgender women (gender discrimination), but have many experiences that are unique.

Trans Status Discrimination

In the field of sociology, Ridgeway defines "status beliefs" as "shared cultural schemas about the status position in society of groups such as those based on gender, race, ethnicity, education, or occupation" (Ridgeway 2001: 637). While a wealth of literature exists that documents the status beliefs attached to cisgender men and cisgender women, very little of this literature conceptualizes "transgender" and "cisgender" as an intersecting axis of status (Deaux and Kite 1993; Eagly 1987; Moss-Racusin et al. 2010; Williams and Best 1982).

In its simplest form, we can ask ourselves, "Are trans people seen as inherently higher-positioned or lower-positioned in society compared to cisgender people, all things equal?" Existing research on this question aside, we can directly explore this through the interviewees' experiences. We looked specifically at situations where the only moving parts occurring at the time concerned trans status. That way, we are more confident that if any discrimination occurred, it was trans status—not any of the many potential other explanations—that contributed to it.

Kai's experiences may fit this bill. When Kai, a white transmasculine person in his thirties, was working in Arizona, he would be on the cusp of employment when the offer would be rescinded. Kai explains, "I get to the HR area and I give them my driver's license [and] my social security . . . they go in the back with whoever just hired me and then they come back out and be like, 'I'm really sorry. We can't offer you this job any longer.'" It appears that, for the interviewers, simply knowing that the gender marked on Kai's legal documents does not match his perceived gender during the interview is enough to invalidate Kai's extreme competence for the position. There are few interpretations of why this may be so. The first is that the disparity between document and interaction was perceived as deceit and dishonesty, and it was this perception of deceit that led to the outcome. The second is that this disparity signaled a certain type of identity which we might call "trans," and that this signaling tapped into negative trans status beliefs. The third is that both of these interpretations are correct to some extent, though the exact details of which cannot be known.

Blake, a mixed trans man in his twenties, experienced something similar when he worked at a video game store. The company hired a new general manager who, as Blake explains, "ruled by fear." Yet, over time Blake was able to befriend this manager and they developed a good working relationship. "He came by the floor a few times and was really nice to me—and of course was an ass to everybody else." This all changed when that manager went into Blake's file to change his pay rate. Immediately after, the manager began subtly challenging Blake's gender. This manager began intentionally misgendering Blake, saying things like "she—I mean, *Blake*, sorry." One time, when Blake was lifting boxes, the manager said, "Why don't you get some manly help back there?" The friendly relationship that Blake had cultivated with this manager evaporated. Blake was told that his manager said during a meeting, "I'm not used to San Francisco faggots out here," and was warned that he was in line to be demoted, and then fired. After learning that Blake was trans, his general manager suddenly began to delegitimize his masculinity (as if a trans masculinity was less genuine than a cisgender masculinity) and delegitimize his gender identity itself (as if Blake's former identity was more genuine than his current one).

Kelly, Alex, Taylor, Casey, and Brett all spoke about trans status beliefs during their interviews. Kelly, a white trans woman in her sixties, matter-of-factly stated that "people don't hire transsexuals [*sic*] ... if they got a choice, why take the queer when you got a perfectly good something else?" This statement suggests that trans status carries with it negative status beliefs. Alex, a white trans woman in her forties, was told by a senior recruiter, "Don't bother going through any recruiters because they're not going to touch you because you're trans ... If they present a candidate that has any deficiencies it reflects on them as a recruiter." Finally, Casey, an indigenous nonbinary person in their twenties, described an experience where their hiring manager seemed to hold these beliefs in an interview. "I let the hiring manager know during my interview I'm transgender and she said ... ' I don't think that's something anybody needs to know.' "

Brett, a white trans man in his twenties, mentioned hiding his trans status while teaching at an elementary school. "My concerns were things like teachers assuming that there were some perversions in it. Parents assuming that there was inherently something sexual to it, wondering if parents would pull their students from school." From Brett's story, we might hypothesize the following: trans status beliefs link being transgender or gender-diverse, as opposed to cisgender, to deficits in competence as well as deficits in character: dishonesty, untrustworthiness, and sexual deviance. *In other words, all else equal, a trans person compared to a cisgender person is seen to be less competent, less worthy of respect, less honest, less trustworthy, and more deviant.* Trans status discrimination is any discrimination that results from these negative status beliefs about trans people.

There might yet be other explanations, however. Casey, an indigenous nonbinary person in their twenties, seemed to articulate this same idea of trans status discrimination when they said, "given two resumes, one of a perfectly 'normal woman' and one of a 'I'm this crazy gender that you don't understand,' if they had both the same level of experience, if both did the same interview, I'm pretty sure the regular person would get the job." Yet, Casey attributed this not to trans status discrimination, but to simple unfamiliarity. "They're more of a known quantity," Casey elaborated, suggesting that perhaps some portion of discrimination results in people simply not understanding what trans means—whether or not they hold negative status beliefs about trans identity.

Gender Discrimination

Differences in status between cisgender men and cisgender women play a major role in the different ways trans men and trans women are treated, as individuals decide appropriate treatment for trans people according to the appropriate treatment for their cisgender counterparts. The workplace experiences of trans men and trans women therefore vary dramatically.

Schilt (2006, 2010) finds that some trans men, both those who are open about their trans status and those who are stealth, are granted greater authority, competency, respect, recognition, prestige, and reward from coworkers, employers, and customers after transitioning in the workplace. However, shorter trans men and trans men of color receive fewer benefits than do tall trans men and white trans men, which "demonstrates that while hegemonic masculinity is defined against femininity, it is also measured against subordinated forms of masculinity" (Schilt 2006: 486). Importantly, trans men who were not using hormones saw little benefit from transitioning, either because they were still viewed as women, as evidenced by coworkers' continued use of feminine pronouns in reference to them, or because they appeared to be quite young due to a lack of facial hair. In other words, Schilt hypothesizes that the benefit from transition is less so a benefit born out of a change in *identity* and more a benefit born out a change in *external perception*. Trans men were able to obtain many of the privileges of masculinity because they were perceived to be men—a feat that was often accomplished with the help of masculinizing HRT.

Trans women, on the other hand, typically lose all the privileges of masculinity after transitioning, and then some. Despite having the same human capital after transitioning, Connell (2009) found that many of the trans women she interviewed felt devalued in the workplace after they transitioned while many of the trans men felt a newly gained sense of privilege. Schilt and Wiswall (2008) found that many trans women experience a loss of authority and pay and are often subject to harassment and termination while many trans men experience an increase in respect, in authority, and occasionally in earnings. Some of that discrimination they encounter is traditional gender discrimination due to a loss of male privilege, as they are no longer perceived to be cisgender men and therefore forgo access to the advantages being a man in the labor market provides.

Like cisgender men, trans men face a less complicated equation for achieving success in the workplace. Since being more masculine is an advantage with regard to ability to access male privilege, the more trans men can display appropriate masculinity, the more likely it is that they will be treated like cisgender men and experience an increase in privilege. In order for trans men to experience an increase in privilege, they must perform hegemonic masculinity through both their physical presentation and behavior.

There are several important aspects of gender expression to consider. Clothing is one, as are the accessories and jewelry one wears, the presence or absence of makeup, and the way one cuts and styles their hair. Masculine-appearing faces tend to have squarer jaws, more pronounced brow bones, and larger noses, while feminine-appearing faces tend to have rounder chins, more pronounced cheekbones, and more vertical rather than backward-sloping foreheads. Height, body mass and muscular composition, and pitch of voice are other key gender markers. Secondary sex characteristics, most noticeably facial hair, an Adam's apple, and breasts, are often seen as signals as to the assigned sex and gender at birth of a given person; it is assumed that only AMAB people can have low voices, facial hair, and body hair, while only AFAB people can have breasts and wider hips; it is these assumptions that allow many trans people who go on HRT to pass as a binary gender.

Verbal interaction style and mannerisms are also important components of gender expression. Those who exhibit a more masculine interactional style are assertive, direct, and dominating; offer their opinion when it isn't requested; and are inclined to interrupt others. Those who exhibit a more feminine style are descriptive, phrase statements as questions, ask others for their opinion, inflect at the end of sentences, and are socioemotional, meaning they focus on the development and maintenance of affective ties. Mannerisms, including the way someone sits, stands, walks, and gestures, are also fundamental cues of gender. People with masculine mannerisms generally take up more physical space and assume power poses (Huang et al. 2011). They tend to sit with their legs spread apart or with their ankle crossed over their knee, stand with their weight evenly distributed across their feet and their feet spread wide, and walk leading with their chest and their arms swinging close to their sides. People with feminine mannerisms generally take up less space. They sit with their legs crossed over the knee or at their ankles, stand with their weight shifted to one foot and a hand on their hip, and walk swaying their hips, allowing their arms to swing loosely. Additionally, people with feminine mannerisms tend to gesture more with their hands when they talk. It is important to note that the gendered nature of mannerisms is certainly not a binary either/or. Many people can and do mix masculine and feminine interactional styles, whether or not they are trans or gender-diverse.

Many trans people choose to undergo hormone replacement therapy, or HRT, in order to both feel more comfortable with their own bodies and intentionally influence others' perceptions of them. For trans men, taking testosterone—masculinizing HRT—will cause facial and body hair to grow, possible male-patterned balding, a deepening of the voice, increased muscle mass and upper body strength, and a redistribution of body fat from the hips to the waist. In addition to HRT, trans men who are not limited by finances may choose to undergo top surgery (mastectomy) and masculinizing facial or body surgery. When costs are not prohibitive, trans women may seek out a variety of transition procedures, including breast augmentation, feminizing facial and body surgery, slimming of the Adam's apple, electrolysis or laser hair removal, and voice therapy.

For trans women, taking estrogen—feminizing HRT—will slow the growth of facial and body hair, reverse male-pattern balding, decrease muscle mass and increase body fat, redistribute fat to a more feminine pattern, cause some nipple and breast growth, and soften the skin. Passing as cisgender can be difficult for a trans woman who started HRT later in life after many masculine secondary sex characteristics have already developed. Passing can be particularly challenging for trans women with deep voices, taller and broader trans women, and trans women who have large hands or feet. HRT does not change the pitch of trans women's voices if they have already experienced puberty, and often significant vocal therapy is needed to change not only pitch but also timbre, tone, and inflection of trans women's voices (Gorham-Rowan and Morris 2006; Neumann and Welzel 2004; Van Borsel, Janssens, and De Bodt 2009).

Johnson, Freeman, and Parker make the interesting argument that because "male" is the dominant sex category in society, a person can be seen as female only when they cannot be categorized as male (2012). Because this sex categorization is often the basis for interpreting others' gender identities, they argue that it thus requires more gender markers to perceive someone as a woman than it does to perceive someone as a man. The implications for binary-identifying trans people are that trans women face more obstacles to passing as cisgender compared to trans men, who after taking hormones are generally perceived as men regardless of conflicting sex signifiers. In fact, Dozier (2005) finds that the presence of facial hair is enough to override other feminine sex characteristics, including having a high voice, breasts, or even being nine months pregnant. Additionally, the drop in trans men's voice pitch due to hormone treatment is itself enough to lead to their passing as cisgender, though they are often read as gay (Zimman 2013). Rory, a Latinx nonbinary person in their twenties, astutely

notes, "Looking at how the world is set up, it's set up for the masculine. Someone who ... present as this ambiguous form, it's safer to
assume that [they are] masculine than ... feminine. Because the world
is set up that way and also I would assume that people have a perception that a woman being called 'sir' would be less insulting than a man
being called 'ma'am.' " For these reasons, if someone is unsure of
another's gender, they will likely tend to assume the person is a man.

TRANS WOMEN

The quality of treatment a trans woman receives is almost entirely
dependent on her ability to "pass," or to be perceived as a cisgender
woman. Because of the binary construction of gender in our society,
failure to be categorized as a woman instantly results in categorization
as a man, making the work of passing risky and difficult. When trans
women are categorized as men, their feminine gender expression often
means that they are additionally categorized as cross-dressers or
transvestites.

Almost every trans women interviewed recounted experiences of
being categorized in this way, most often by cisgender men who view
them to be "deviant" men. We use the term "deviant" with extreme
caution and we must restate nonpassing trans women do not identify
as men, nor is their gender identity and expression immoral. Nevertheless, many cisgender men who interact with nonpassing trans
women do so on the basis of the belief that they are men, and that they
embody a deviant masculinity. Deviant masculinity can be thought of
as one of the most subordinate of masculinities, and a form of masculinity that faces the most intense gender policing, prejudice, and hostility from cisgender men embodying hegemonic masculinity.

Passing is more than a strategy used by trans women who wish to be
categorized as women. On the level of the individual, gender expression is often a means to arrive at greater authenticity and comfort.
Trans people often modify their gender expression for their own benefit to perform gender in a way that aligns with their gender identities.
However, any gender expression results in reactions from other social
actors—social actors who may hold more or less rigid gender beliefs,
and respond more or less well to perceived violations. Trans women
must thus make difficult choices between authenticity at the risk of
repercussions, or avoid discrimination at the cost of emotional and
mental well-being. Important to note too is the significant financial
and time investment required for the social, medical, and legal transitions that many trans women pursue. The high barrier to entry to

living authentically as another gender may preclude many trans women from coming out altogether.

Many of the trans women who were interviewed experienced a drastic drop in workplace treatment as they transitioned away from being perceived as conventionally masculine men. The loss of male privilege—and perhaps the additional stigma of negative trans status beliefs—has led to a significant increase in difficulty finding employment, conflict in interpersonal interactions, and a loss in respect and perceived competency in the workplace for all but one trans woman interviewed. None of the six trans women in my study experienced gains in their quality of workplace treatment to the extent that the trans men did, when such gains happened at all. The reason for this disparity in treatment centers on societal perception of gender expression.

Taylor, a white trans woman in her thirties, decided to transition and began hormone therapy after moving to San Francisco at the age of 30. Taylor was critical of her appearance, saying "[People often characterize me as] cross dresser and a tranny or a transsexual . . . I think I don't have passability as a female just by physical appearance." Taylor identified her facial features as the major reason why she believed others categorized her as a cross-dressing man. "I even get 'him' when I have makeup and my finger nails painted . . . when people . . . just make an assumption on facial features I think it just triggers them whether it's subconsciously or consciously into using male pronouns and, so that's a reason behind [wanting] a facial feminization jaw [surgery]." Her speech was also a characteristic that contributed to others categorizing her as a man. "I'm not opposed to doing speech interventions to make my voice more feminine because I get clocked on the phone all the time as male and some people will say, especially children, 'but your voice sounds a man!'" If it were up to Taylor, she would not undergo more transition procedures. "I'm already pretty comfortable with myself," Taylor explained. Her main motivation for wanting these procedures was "to be stealth." Taylor was exhausted with the prejudice she received for being trans. "I just want people to leave me alone, [to] stop saying things." Taylor's experiences exemplify the complicated decisions trans people must make between their own comfort and the external experiences of discrimination they receive.

Taylor was well aware of how her privilege as a "white educated male" worked in her favor prior to transitioning. One of Taylor's first jobs, when she was still perceived as a man, was at a fast food restaurant. "My starting salary was more than one of the women who was there a year. They offered me pretty much to be on the track to be district manager, they wanted me there every minute." She felt like since transitioning, her salaries in her jobs in the education field are noticeably lower, which she can attribute to no other reason. "In all my jobs I've gone down in salary instead of up . . . I have to work more overtime." One job experience she spoke about illustrates negative trans status beliefs. When Taylor taught about gendered pronouns in a Hebrew class, a parent accused her of trying to negatively influence children. "The parent calls me over . . . as if I'm trying to corrupt them with male/female stuff and I was so embarrassed [and] uncomfortable . . . I had to sit there and oh, really explain for ten minutes that [gendered nouns are] part of Hebrew and that this is not about . . . I'm not trying to 'trans your child' or something." The parent expressed suspicion that Taylor's identity as trans was both deviant and predatory, an assumption that caused Taylor significant distress.

Robin, a white trans woman in her fifties, had been on HRT for about three years at the time of the interview. Strangers rarely used "sir" when addressing Robin, but Robin was often clocked as both trans and as a cross-dressing man. While the line between the two couldn't be more clear to Robin, she noted that it may be fuzzier to others. "There is the commonly held belief of what a transsexual is— I mean, they know what the technical definition of the transsexual is, but then we say transgender, and they think of the most visible representations that they've seen most often, which is drag queens and cross-dressers. And they don't understand that those are men . . . and this is different." Robin put significant effort into changing her physical and behavioral presentation. Robin noticed that the more feminine her gender expression, the better she was treated. "I wear far more makeup than any other woman does . . . [because] the more female clues to my gender I can give them the less they see as a man." She adjusted her clothing to provide further gender cues, and took advantage of the fact that "business casual for women is a lot different than it is for men." Robin consciously modified her body language and mannerisms so that she is read as more feminine. "Instead of just bending over at the waist to grab something, I'll just squat down and grab it that way. [I'll stand with] hands on the hips, keeping my arms in closer, just basically general physical mannerisms that are female." Robin has not had speech therapy, but used her past as a vocalist to help her manipulate her voice. She pointed out that, "It's not just putting on a dress and wearing makeup. To me, it wasn't just learning to talk in a higher voice. It's the words, women use different words than guys do. There is a different inflection, there is a different cadence to it all and it's hard, you have to think about it a lot . . . the higher up and the softer I get with my voice, the less misgendering I get." Robin spoke little about whether any of these efforts personally helped her feel authentic as a woman, however.

Unlike Taylor, Robin worked in a male-dominated union job as an audio technician. It was easy for Robin to see the way male privilege operates in her industry. "When I see a set of crew go into a ballroom where they're setting up the head table, microphones and console, if it's a male and female, nine times out of ten the guy will go to the console, start patching things in and settings things and taking control and operating the system [and] start . . . taking authority, unless the woman has had more experience, who's been in the Union longer, and has just learned that if you want to do the jobs, you got to have to stand up and take them because the guys won't give it to you." Robin was able to see the ways in which the women in the union were held to a higher standard. "Their work is always scrutinized a lot more closer . . . the female engineers have to be a lot more precise, and a lot more through in what they do and so they are perceived as taking more time, nitpicking, and worrying about little things. She just can't do it fast enough." Robin experienced a sharp decline in workplace respect and authority since she has transitioned to a feminine presentation. She was unable to get as many high-paying jobs, was assigned less work overall, and was more highly critiqued for the work she did. The fact that Robin was more disadvantaged compared to when she was perceived as a man suggests a loss of male privilege and that at least part of the inequality she was experiencing was the typical discrimination many cisgender women face. However, Robin reflected that since transitioning she was treated worse than her cisgender women coworkers and she was unable to get the same quantity or quality of jobs that they could. Additionally, Robin faced intentional misgendering and trans-specific harassment from her supervisor and coworkers. Robin experienced both standard gender discrimination and trans discrimination, and was thus highly disadvantaged in her workplace compared to before she transitioned.

Kelly, a white trans woman in her sixties, began transitioning later in life and has undergone an extensive series of surgeries, including facial feminization. She was on hormone therapy for four years at the time of the interview. Kelly presented "extremely feminine" in dress and accessories, and wore bold makeup. Kelly believed her body language and gesturing were read as more quintessentially feminine than most cisgender women. However, Kelly described her verbal interaction style as extremely masculine and as a characteristic that often leads others to clock her as trans. Kelly spoke of her "stainless steel self-confidence." She regarded her level of aggression in the workplace as antagonistic now that others perceived her as a woman. "I guess I have a very male presentation in work situations and the men get really intimidated by it because women normally don't pound their fist and say, 'You're full of shit!' " Encountering the backlash cisgender women face for being too agentic, Kelly experienced difficulty navigating the fine line of combining communal and agentic behavior in a way in which she was perceived as competent and yet still likable.

Kelly, an architect, found that the incongruity between her feminine physical presentation and masculine-sounding voice made it difficult for her to obtain work. "My business card . . . has a photo of me as a woman on it, I looked really good in it so [employers] just assumed I was a woman until somebody had to interview me." Since transitioning, Kelly has had difficulty finding work as potential employers feared she would scare away clients. " 'You brought a guy in a dress' is what he's afraid [customers are] going to say." Another potential employer was explicit about his fears of hiring Kelly to work for him. "He got a client that he was going to lose the project on because he was unqualified for it. He did not have the experience, professional experience. I have it in spades. He had a decision to make. He says, 'If I hire you, I got to take you and meet with these people and I'm afraid that you're a transsexual, you're going to kill this job for me if I take you to them.' " In Kelly's experience, either individuals perceived her as a cross-dressing man and sanctioned her on the basis of her "deviant masculinity," or they perceived her as a trans woman and sanctioned her on the basis of trans status discrimination.

Alex, a white trans woman in her forties, had been on hormone therapy for two and half years at the time of interview. Alex's more feminine gender expression consisted of wearing skirts or dresses and heels all of the time. Alex has had many feminization surgeries, including breast augmentation, brow surgery, and work on her jaw and chin. Although Alex "never once out in public [gets] anything other than female pronouns," she said, "[I don't believe] anyone . . . thinks I'm anything other than trans [but I] project how I expect to be gendered very clearly to people." Alex has undergone speech therapy, yet identifies that phone interviews are difficult for her due to her voice being the only gendered cue interviewers receive. "The voice is the problem because . . . when I get misgendered is on the phone. It [is] frustrating because when I meet people face-to-face my ability to communicate confidence is much better face to face than anything over the phone." Alex consciously feminized the way she stands and walks. "I stand straighter and more compactly. Legs closer together, arms closer together . . . attempting to not slump as best I can." Alex acknowledged that her verbal interactional style did not change since transitioning, admitting that she was still assertive, offered her opinion even when it wasn't asked for, and was prone to interrupting others.

Alex painfully felt the loss of her male privilege. "There are times where I think, whether real or imagined, I don't feel like I get treated as well as I did when I was a very privileged white male . . . I have so little tolerance for not being treated correctly and yet I don't feel that I've been treated seriously. I mean, I had a couple of situations recently where I really felt like I was being kind of brushed off as just kind of a blonde airhead." Ales spoke extensively and insightfully on the explicit trans status discrimination that occurs during the hiring process for executive-level positions. She recounted how she was told by a senior recruiter, "Don't bother going through any recruiters because they're not going to touch you because you're trans . . . If they present a candidate that has any deficiencies it reflects on them as a recruiter." It was clear to Alex that being trans was a negative mark on her resume, and a large one at that. Alex was in a challenging situation in which her extensive experience in executive-level positions conflicted with her status as a woman, and especially her status as a trans woman. Employment became elusive for her.

Whitney, a white trans woman in her twenties, had been on feminizing HRT for a year and a half at the time of the interview. Whitney was unhappy about her inability to always pass as cisgender, noting that "there might be empathy for somebody that's not passing, there's also a lot of ridicule." Whitney saw herself moving toward an increasingly feminine presentation, finances permitting, in order to mitigate difficulties associated with not passing. "It's a financial thing always, I mean because I don't pass as cis and because it's easier to live in a world where you're considered cisgender. I want to get like facial feminization surgery and things along those lines." Whitney described her mannerisms as calm and low-key, purposefully not attention-seeking or outgoing. "I mean I'm more reserved. I'm not boisterous in my expressions. I guess I just try to be invisible." Although Whitney expressed her gender in more feminine ways, she explored with various gender presentations in her unsuccessful attempts to obtain a job in the male-dominated industry of machinery. By varying hairstyle, clothing, and makeup, Whitney went to some interviews presenting masculine, some presenting feminine, and some presenting androgynous. To Whitney, a feminine presentation included "totally women's clothes, bra and . . . maybe a darker eyeliner [and] mascara." Presenting masculine involved "hair in a ponytail and no makeup and wearing guy clothes." An androgynous presentation to Whitney included "tighter cut clothing . . . wearing [my hair] down and a little bit styled" and "very light [makeup] . . . almost indistinguishable from no makeup." Whitney found that when presenting androgynously or on the masculine side of the spectrum, her person was scrutinized more than her abilities. When presenting feminine, interviewers were friendlier but she still wasn't able to obtain a job.

Whitney experienced discrimination both before and after she began her transitioning to a more feminine gender expression. Before transitioning, she was perceived as a shy, effeminate man and was often harassed. Before starting HRT, she began presenting in more feminine ways in her manufacturing job, the most visible of which was growing out her hair and wearing makeup. Her manager immediately noticed. "My hair was about shoulder length at the time and kept bugging me and joking me about getting a haircut and stuff like that. I was starting to get giggles and stuff because I wear like eyeliner and a little bit of makeup." Over time, Whitney began feeling like she was receiving increased scrutiny and less independence over her job and had her input increasingly ignored.

She was eventually laid off after six or seven months, one week after having begun HRT. She experienced significant difficulties in obtaining employment after, despite her efforts to modify her gender expression in order to become employable. While working in manufacturing, Whitney was categorized as having a subordinate or deviant masculinity for her long hair and makeup, and was teased and belittled accordingly. While applying for new jobs, Whitney's experimenting with different gender expressions was a comprehensive yet unsuccessful attempt to reobtain employment. "[My gender expression] is really the only thing that's changed. In the past trying to get a position in a machine shop was pretty easy. I could find a job within a month or two." It may be that when Whitney was presenting more masculine, her demeanor categorized her as a subordinate masculinity, and when Whitney was presenting more feminine, trans status discrimination and gender discrimination (manufacturing is a highly gendered profession) became salient. The double bind that Whitney faced here led to a long spell of unemployment that prompted her to leave the industry for good.

Leslie, a white trans woman in her thirties, financially invested much into her transition including electrolysis and several feminization surgeries. At the time of the interview, she had been on HRT for four years, which she said, "[caused] some fat redistribution on my face" and "decent breast development" as well as the feeling that "more [of] my emotions were accessible." Leslie reported passing almost always as a cisgender woman, with strangers almost never using "sir" when addressing her. For Leslie, the effort she invested into creating a more feminine gender expression peaked when she first began transitioning, but has since lowered. "Earlier in my transition, especially right after I went full-time [as a woman], I did dress more overtly female . . . I wore makeup daily after I transitioned . . . [now] I tend not to wear it very often." Leslie used to study mannerisms as well, though these eventually became second-nature for her. "I would be more like legs straight together and hands under the table. [I would pay attention to] how I walk and how I move and how I gesture . . . [there are] a thousand and one different things that I noted and emulated . . . it eventually becomes background, but there are distinctly two sets of motions with male and femaleness." Leslie enlisted the help of her workers to craft her gender expression, inviting them openly to "discreetly pull me aside and feel free to let me know" when her actions or gestures were perceived as masculine.

Leslie was the only trans woman we spoke to who encountered very little discrimination, saying, "I don't feel like I've lost a huge degree of male privilege." Leslie attributes this lack of discrimination to her advanced education and the professional nature of her job. "As far as workplace discrimination goes, I didn't really get a lot of flak on anything because . . . I don't work in a blue-collar area. I work with scientists, with people who are degreed, etcetera. I'm not trying to be like ivory tower here, but it's like there is a different mindset than you would find at McDonalds or in a factory or something like that." While there was undoubtedly some truth to Leslie's assessments, education and a professional career do not shield many trans women from discrimination, as Alex's experiences demonstrate. An important factor in the lack of discrimination Leslie faced may be the culture created by her company's well-established trans-friendly policies and explicit condemnation of trans discrimination. Another factor contributing to Leslie's positive experience may have been the explicitness with which she sought out help to pass better in the workplace. By doing so, she may have signaled her strong desire to be seen as a cisgender woman, and thus avoided being categorized as a cross-dressing man.

The Big Ideas

- In general, every trans woman interviewed—with the notable exception of Leslie—experienced a noticeable drop in their perceived competence, respect, honesty, and trustworthiness after transitioning.
- While every trans woman interviewed took efforts to pass as a cisgender woman after transition, they enjoyed different levels of success due to factors like age at transition and access to transition procedures like feminizing HRT, speech therapy, and facial feminization surgery.

- The most striking experiences of discrimination occurred for those trans women who were perceived by others, for whatever reason, to be cross-dressing men. These individuals faced heavy social sanctioning and discrimination due to this perceived "deviant masculinity" that has all but kept them unemployed.
- Some trans women were perceived as *neither* cross-dressing men *nor* cisgender women. This suggests that "trans woman" is its own perceptual category, with its own attached status beliefs and stereotypes.
- Trans status beliefs are overwhelmingly negative, and include less competent, less worthy of respect, less honest, less trustworthy, and more deviant. These beliefs may be as negative as they are due to trans women being doubly sanctioned for embracing femininity (lower status) and leaving masculinity (higher status).
- Trans women, if perceived as trans women and not cross-dressing men, must reckon with *both* classic gender discrimination that privileges men and masculinity over women and femininity *and* trans status discrimination.

TRANS MEN

For trans men, the treatment they receive is contingent on their ability to be seen as "one of the guys" (Schilt 2006, 2010). To gain entry to this privileged category, trans men must sufficiently embody the high standards of hegemonic masculinity through their physical characteristics and mannerisms. If successful, they receive huge increases in their perceived respect and competence and are granted entry into men's circles. Trans men who do not pass as men and are perceived instead as women do not have access to advantages experienced by passing trans men. Instead, their manhood is almost unilaterally delegitimized, Trans men who pass as men yet embodied a subordinate masculinity also have their masculinity teased, berated, and delegitimized as a form of social pressure to conform to hegemonic masculinity—in much the same way that cisgender men embodying subordinate masculinities experience.

Perhaps the most comprehensive example of the potential benefits of hegemonic masculinity can be seen in Parker's story. As an interviewee, Parker, a white trans man in his twenties, was remarkably meticulous about describing all of the changes he experienced in the workplace, and so we include much of his analysis here.

Parker had been on hormones for about two years at the time of the interview and was almost always read as a cisgender man. Strangers used "sir" all the time when they addressed him. Parker considered himself to still be in the process of transitioning and remained conscious of the gendered implications of his mannerisms, including hand gestures, sitting positions, and standing stances. "I had a professor in undergrad that kind of talked about girls tending to sit cross legged and taking up the minimum amount of space possible. I think that has stuck with me a lot so, I try not to do that if I catch myself doing it" and so he consciously tries to "sit kind of masculine." Parker felt that sometimes he would "come off as a little stiff" in conversation because of his heightened awareness of his own tendency to adopt the other person's mannerisms in conversations, which he perceived as a more feminine trait. However, since people began to consistently recognize him as a man, Parker was able to relax some of his efforts and learned to display masculinity more naturally. Parker was very intentional about learning to present in a masculine way, making it easier for others to perceive him as a man.

Parker transitioned from a butch woman to a trans man while working as a sales analyst, and did so seamlessly, thanks to an established transition policy laid out by HR. Parker reported being accepted "instantly in the boys club." Once a part of the boy's club, Parker was easily able to access male privilege. "I was shocked at how instantly, especially with male colleagues, the hurdles of being a [butch] woman in the workplace fell down . . . So for the male colleagues, I'm a voice. I say something and it goes . . . I have to be careful about what I say, because if I say something, no one fights me about it. They say okay and they go for it." Parker was granted more agency and influence in his job. "I still have the same job title but my responsibilities have grown. I think they were very related to gender changes and the way that I'm viewed with the company . . . I have a lot more opportunities, I have had several promotions in the last year, pay raises, and a lot more opportunity to explore more things. And, most importantly, more say about what opportunities I get. So I don't just get handed gifts, I get to talk about where do I want to go and what do I want to do. Things like that definitely didn't have before."

Parker acknowledged the improved treatment he has received since transitioning with some unease. "There are a lot of things, there a lot of privileges that I have inherited that I feel a little uncomfortable with because they are real, and they are odd to deal with because I might not have the best idea in the room and I'm not used to thinking that I do." Yet, even with his newfound awareness, Parker at times found himself included in instances of workplace sexism and exclusion. Parker explained that one time, "There was a young attractive girl that had been moved into the office across from me, she was very sweet. My boss kind of came by and just said 'I did that for you.'" In this situation, though Parker had never asked for it, he was included in a sexist and objectifying masculine camaraderie that reinforced the exclusivity of men's spaces.

Since Parker has constant and complete access to male privilege in the workplace, he experienced the freedom to exhibit both feminine and masculine characteristics in a way that felt authentic. "I'd like to be able to judge each situation that I'm in and really just act the way that I feel is appropriate, whether that involves masculine [tendencies] like charging full force [or feminine ones like] being able to compromise." Parker noticed that, as a man, he no longer had to navigate the complicated challenge of combining agency and communality to achieve success that many women struggle with in the workplace. "I was especially in workplaces aggressive [as a butch woman]. I wanted to make sure that my opinion was heard and I think in some ways, it might have held me back because I became combative. But also I feel like if I did show sort of feminine characteristics I was absolutely over washed versus now [as] a male suggesting these kinds of compromises and things I'm more heard and I'm allowed to embody those kinds of things now." Parker's experiences demonstrate the substantial increase in workplace treatment that is possible for individuals who transition to and pass successfully into the narrow range of hegemonic masculinity. Furthermore, his experiences suggest a hierarchy of gender in which not only are men who embody hegemonic masculinity privileged over all women, but also butch women are privileged over feminine women.

Kai, a white transmasculine person in his thirties, had been on HRT for seven years and had top surgery, both of which allowed him to pass easily as a cisgender man, with strangers addressing him with "sir" about 90 percent of the time. He wore men's clothing exclusively and sometimes wore facial hair. Kai was able to pass because "[I am] tall and my voice doesn't sound like a normal trans-man voice. I have a pretty fluid voice which I'm very lucky about and I just present extremely male usually." However, Kai did not "made any conscious effort to change" his mannerisms and he believed that while his mannerisms appeared masculine when he was perceived to be a butch woman they started to appear effeminate. "How I'm presenting, like my mannerisms just exactly right now, are the same mannerisms I had when I presented as a stone butch . . . [but] now [I] appear to be a flaming gay man." In addition to gesturing, Kai maintained other feminine mannerisms. "I still cross my legs like a girl when I don't think about it. I do it all of the time and men look at me so weird." Kai's standing posture and walking style exhibited qualities from "both sides of the spectrum." "If I'm really happy, I sashay and I don't mean to. [But also] I can walk very firmly. I can walk very like, 'Get the hell out of my way!' "

Unlike Parker, Kai had a career marked by extreme cases of harassment and overt discrimination, especially *since* transitioning. A major factor contributing to the discrimination that Kai faced was that much of his work experience took place in the more conservative state of Arizona, which does not provide statewide legal employment protection for trans individuals. When Kai told his boss he was transitioning in his work as an ophthalmologist, his boss assured him that there would be no problems. "We had come to the fact that I was transitioning and that it would not affect my job. I wasn't going to do anything crazy. I wasn't going to try to grow facial hair, and I didn't really have any. I was not going to make the clients uncomfortable, basically I was just going to continue to present as myself . . . two or three days later, I was removed from my position as management . . . He basically made my entire life hell at work." Kai was demoted, given a pay reduction, and put on an unsustainable work schedule. His boss no longer allowed him to participate in continuing education opportunities and severely reduced his responsibilities in the workplace. The discrimination was so intolerable that Kai quit and decided to change career paths and obtain a certified nursing assistant license.

Although being well qualified for many positions as a hospice nurse, Kai was repeatedly experienced being almost hired or immediately fired when his inconsistent documents outed his trans history. Despite having "an amazing resume," Kai said he was told that he couldn't be hired "probably 20 times in four months." It was not Kai's masculine appearance in a female-dominated industry that prevented him from obtaining a job; rather it was his inconsistent paperwork that outed him as a trans person. Despite clearly having the qualifications for all of these jobs he applied to, trans status discrimination worked to immediately disqualify Kai from any and all of these positions. Despite these frustrating and hurtful experiences, Kai refused to change his driver's license to say that he was male because he "wanted to educate people . . . because people need to learn." When Kai finally found a place that would hire him, his employers took advantage of him by overworking and underpaying him because they knew he was desperate for a job. Kai said he was treated "like a leper," and his boss would verbally harass him in an effort to delegitimize his masculinity, telling Kai he was not manly enough and often calling him a "nelly." This experience is an example in which Kai faced both trans status discrimination and gender discrimination, as his subordinate masculinity was constantly mocked.

Kai left Arizona for California in hopes of finding a more trans-friendly workplace. Kai enjoyed his current job, where he was assured his trans identity would be a nonissue, and Kai said he felt respected. However, while he had great relations with his immediate boss, Kai had some conflict with the owner of the company, who "is in his 70s and calls himself basically a rehab chauvinist pig." The owner delegitimized Kai's masculinity by referring to him as a "pretend man," which Kai said, "keeps him comfortable and not threatened [because] he still gets to be the man. I think it's a control thing with him." It is difficult, however, to disentangle what may be both trans status discrimination and gender discrimination. Did the owner believe that Kai's trans status makes him "not a man," and thus a woman? Or, did the owner believe that Kai's appearance as a gay man make him "not a man" on the basis of being a subordinate masculinity? It is entirely possible that Kai was not experiencing trans discrimination specifically but rather more general discrimination against nonhegemonic masculinity.

Blake, a mixed trans man in his twenties, was always read as a man and never had strangers never address him as "ma'am." At 5'6" and under 120 pounds, Blake said he "got made fun of because I was . . . smaller." His small stature along with his youthful appearance served as a frustrating hindrance to his acceptance by other men in the workplace. Blake's stature was further minimized by his tendency to hunch over, body language that formed from years of trying to hide his chest. Blake did not put too much thought into the way he sat, stood, or walked, although he did pay attention to correcting his occasional habit of crossing his legs in a feminine way. Blake was generally not a very assertive person and his demeanor was not stereotypically masculine, which further hindered his ability to access male privilege. Blake had been on HRT for two years at the time of the interview, but other than providing a deeper voice and facial hair, his physical presentation remained largely the same. However, Blake's self-esteem did change "Because I started binding and in the last couple of years because of the [testosterone], I'm feeling more comfortable with how I look generally."

While working at a video game store, Blake experienced a clear instance of trans status discrimination. After a new manager was hired, Blake and this manager became good friends and bonded as men in the workplace. "He came by the floor a few times and was really nice to me—and of course was an ass to everybody else." This all changed, however, when that manager went into Blake's file to change his pay rate and read through his paperwork. Immediately afterward, the manager began subtly challenging Blake's gender in the workplace.

One time, when Blake was lifting boxes, the manager said, "Why don't you get some manly help back there?" He began misgendering Blake, saying things like "she—I mean, *Blake*, sorry" when before Blake had never been misgendered. The friendly relationship that Blake had cultivated with this manager evaporated, and Blake was eventually fired from this job.

In other workplaces, Blake faced less trans status discrimination but more gender discrimination due to Blake's small size (according to Blake, he has "been trying very, very hard to bulk up, but that doesn't work well") and inability to do heavy physical labor due to a disability. At an LGBT nonprofit, Blake was harassed for not being able to lift heavy objects due to back problems when one of his cisgender woman employers told him, "If I can do it, you can do it ... man up." At a pet food store, Blake felt his stealth trans status served to disadvantage him because others interpreted his inability to move heavy merchandise as laziness, but he believed they would have more compassion "if they thought I was female." Instead, Blake was often teased when he would try to lift heavy merchandise or reach items on tall shelves. " 'Do we need to get that little man?' or 'You look like you are going to crack a rib' or ... I'm trying to reach something and ... they'll just walk over and stand next to me like, 'Wish you could do that?' "

Brett, a white trans man in his twenties, has not undergone HRT and found his youthful appearance to be particularly challenging in the workplace. "I come off as a lot younger and that's because I do look female while kind of male at the same time ... so that's one thing that I struggle with ... appearing to be ... my actual age, a lot of people kind of say I look like I'm 15." Strangers referred to Brett as "sir" about 45 percent of the time. Brett did not believe he fit the conception of hegemonic masculinity. "I don't consider myself as a male who's a jock, I don't consider myself as tough. I do consider myself a bit nerdy. I mean I don't consider myself macho." He didn't believe he passes as male, and believed strangers addressed him with "sir" about half the time. Brett said, "[I don't pass] entirely as male if we're talking about being stealth, which I actually enjoy. I feel like my hands are very feminine. I think I have a really feminine face. I think I have a very feminine form, like when we're talking about my hips, things like that." Brett would like to "be a little more masculine" and would consider taking testosterone and undergoing top surgery, but for the time being was content engaging in less permanent means of altering his presentation. Brett had to exert conscious efforts to exhibit a more stereotypically masculine communication style at work, and acknowledged the ways in which he was at a disadvantage. "I think that I kind of struggled to be more assertive in my roles, to like present my ideas and ask questions and kind of not just go along with things." Brett believed that being more comfortable with his masculine expression granted him more confidence, which in turn had him excel more at work. "When you think you're looking good one day, you're going to act like more confident. You're going to speak better; you're going to like perform better."

Brett had virtually no experiences with discrimination, which can be attributed to his willingness to be perceived as a butch woman at workplaces where he thought being perceived as a trans man would be a disadvantage, including two nonprofits dedicated to women's rights, and Brett's lack of insistence to be out about his trans identity. When Brett taught at an elementary school, he was worried that coworkers and parents might perceive his trans identity as something deviant, so he remained closeted. "My concerns were things like teachers assuming that there were some perversions in it. Parents assuming that there was inherently something sexual to it, wondering if parents would pull their students from school." Brett attributed his lack of discrimination to his racial and socioeconomic privilege. "I realize a lot of like discrimination I think trans men of color would face, I haven't. And I think that's because of being white and also coming from a really privileged educational background. I think if I didn't have those backgrounds I would be discriminated a lot more."

Brett was the only trans man interviewed who was able to pass as a cisgender woman, and this unique ability was almost certainly due to Brett being the only trans man interviewed who did not undergo masculinizing HRT. Brett's motivations for avoiding masculinizing HRT were that doing so would have put his ability to pass as a cisgender woman at risk. "I think that I also have a privilege of not being clocked as trans . . . a couple of my friends who were on [testosterone] faced a lot more harassment because they're clocked the second you see them. For me, I'm saying 'call me male,' but I don't look a way that [is] threatening . . . and I think that [is] key."

The only job in which Brett felt he received trans discrimination was the only job in which he was out to everyone at work as trans, when he worked in customer service. In that workplace, his coworkers referred to him with feminine pronouns, and worse, with feminine pet names like "little mama." When Brett came out to his coworkers as "male-identified," his coworkers told him "everyone already knows" because he was using the men's restroom. Exacerbating this situation, they chose to continue to misgender him as a woman even after he came out. "It was a terrible experience . . . I think of this place as being really inappropriate." Perhaps because Brett did not pass as a man, his manhood was completely delegitimized in this environment. This significantly hurt his emotional well-being in this workplace, though Brett soon became used to and even appreciative of his ability to be whatever gender people want him to. Brett's experiences were unique because, while his masculinity and identity as a trans man was frequently delegitimized and discounted, this was an outcome that did not bother Brett. This gave him the unique ability to dodge experiences of discrimination that people like Kai or Blake would have experienced in the same situations.

The Big Ideas

- Trans men who transitioned to an acceptable degree of hegemonic masculinity experienced huge gains in perceived respect, competence, opportunities, and authority in the workplace.
- Trans men who were perceived as embodying a subordinate masculinity—whether small and less strong, like Blake, or effeminate and overexpressive, like Kai—faced social sanctions in the workplace from other men.
- While being perceived as a man embodying hegemonic masculinity is unilaterally better than being perceived as any kind of woman, it is unclear whether being perceived as a man embodying subordinate masculinity is necessarily better than being perceived as any kind of woman. While both Kai and Blake expressed that in certain situations, they would have preferred to have been women, it is almost a given that, in other situations, they experience privilege for being seen as men. On the other hand, Brett's ability to be perceived as a woman allowed him to escape many experiences of discrimination that he might have received if perceived as a trans man embodying a subordinate masculinity.

BUTCH WOMEN

Levitt and Hiestand (2004) describe butch identity as both a subjective understanding of individual "womanhood" to be masculine and a performance in which gender is expressed in stereotypically masculine ways. The experiences of butch women are interesting in that they involve both a high-status identity (masculine or butch) and a low-status identity (woman). While people of any gender and any assigned sex at birth may identify as butch, in this book, those masculine or butch women interviewed were all AFAB and perceived as butch women.

We might assume that, compared to feminine women, butch women experience advantages due to possessing an advantaged identity (butch) in the gender hierarchy. Earlier research by Wong, Kettlewell, and Sproule (1985) shows support for this idea, suggesting that masculine women outperformed more feminine women in the workplace. Additionally, not only the presence of masculinity but also the absence of femininity was shown to be a strong predictor of this higher achievement, lending support to the idea that femininity is a negative characteristic in the workplace (763). A butch identity and expression offers certain gendered protection by excusing agentic behavior that might otherwise provoke a backlash effect negatively affecting perceptions of likability or respect (Craig and Lacroix 2011). Other research was more mixed on whether or not butchness was a beneficial identity in the workplace, identifying that some experiences looked like "butchness as a workplace asset" that earned more respect and perceived competence, while other experiences looked more like "workplace harassment, sometimes related to being lesbian and other times to being butch" (Levitt and Hiestand 2004: 616). As this literature is inconclusive, we look closely at the experiences of those interviewees who identified as butch women at the time of the interview, as well as those interviewees who identified as butch women at some point in time.

Pat, a white butch woman in her fifties, enjoyed it when people weren't sure of her gender. To her surprise, strangers used "sir" only about 20 percent of the time, but she noted that when she was younger she would get gendered as a man more frequently. Pat had no desire for HRT although she made conscious efforts to suppress any body language that could be read as feminine. "I don't cross my legs. I always have my legs like apart [. . . I put my hands] in my pockets [. . . and I walk with my] shoulders back and forth . . . I will keep my hands crossed and my arms folded or down [to prevent myself from talking with my hands]." Pat's communication style was more aggressive than that of her cisgender women coworkers—she did not engage in caretaking behavior and was prone to interrupting. Pat's aggressive personality led her to seek out higher-paying, male-dominated positions at the grocery stores where she worked. "I worked as a cashier two days . . . and I was promoted to the POS lead, which is the person in charge of all the prices in the store, all the signage . . . I mean it was a lot of work . . . I realize I always seem to choose the high pressure stuff." Pat was more likely to ask for a raise than any of her coworkers, saying, "I insisted on getting my pay raise and I fought for the pay raise. I fought. I went to the union. I went to the district manager . . . I wasn't afraid to say 'look, this is what's mine, I earned this.' "

It is impossible to determine whether the physical or behavioral aspects of Pat's masculine presentation elevated her into high positions of authority, but it is clear that she was respected and viewed as highly competent. "It's funny, the women would come to me and ask me, 'what do you think of this? How would you do that?' and also the guys do too." There was preferential gender treatment at the grocery store where she worked, however unconscious, as Pat observed that the other "masculine women" would also have their opinion sought after but not any of "the feminine women." Pat experienced pressure to assume managerial positions, similar to the glass escalator effect experienced by men in female-dominated occupations as they are pushed into supervisorial roles (Williams 1992). Despite her lack of interest, Pat was pressured to become management unusually early. "Three years with the company and then wanting to make me management, I mean there's people that started with me [12 years ago] that still aren't in management." After moving to a new grocery store in San Francisco, Pat had to repeatedly turn down offers to be promoted to a position of management. "I'm not going to be promoted. I'm not going to because as soon as I [became] management, I didn't like who I was and I wasn't going to do that here. But I mean, I have been asked probably a dozen times." Pat's experiences speak to the idea that gender discrimination falls less heavily on butch women, compared to feminine women.

Sam, a white and Latinx butch woman in their thirties, transitioned to a more masculine gender presentation after college. Sam chose to refrain from HRT. Although Sam preferred their gender-ambiguous chosen name and gender-neutral pronouns, they used their feminine birth name and feminine pronouns throughout their work history. While strangers used "sir" about 65 percent of the time, Sam's coworkers perceived them to be a butch woman. Sam dressed in masculine clothing at work, saying, "I tend to wear slacks and button down shirts [and] vests and ties with some regularity. Always men's shoes." Sam took up space in the way they move and in their body posture, noting, "even like my shoulders . . . I used to collapse them and now they take up more space." Sam's communication style was direct and aggressive, usually causing them to relate better with men than women in the workplace. "[With] women . . . there's an assumption that there's going to be this kinship of how we communicate on their part and then I try to be really direct and more matter of fact and cold and business oriented and there's clearly a way that it doesn't work for them . . . I've realized I prefer to a certain extent working with men. Largely because of the communication cadence." When asked to further describe their communication obstacles, Sam explained, "I can say something really direct and even sometimes critical . . . with like a guy and it's received in a way without sensitivity. It's usually like, 'Got it. On it. Okay, I hear you.' . . . Whereas the tendency with the women I've worked with has been a lack of receptivity to the directness or the harshness or the coldness of the communication."

The match between Sam's sartorial and verbal presentation was important to their success at work. "There was definitely preference for being the more dominant communicator . . . I'm successful because of my aggressive communication pattern and then there's less resentment or weirdness around it or resistance to it or criticism because of my gender presentation. [When feminine-presenting women use a similar communication style] they get painted as a bitch." A masculine or butch expression offered some backlash protection by excusing agentic behavior that might otherwise negatively affect perceptions of likability for feminine women. However, while Sam was offered more leeway than their feminine presenting coworkers, they were not able to act with total impunity. "My communication patterns at work often, even though they'll be rewarded, I'll also often get general advice about possibly toning it down. So I've developed an awareness because a lot of the times of the feedback. [I'm told] that I'll be really aggressive and I'll be intimidating." Sam received mixed messages because while their forcefulness was rewarded, they were still perceived to be a woman and therefore subject to some backlash for being seen as insufficiently communal. At the same time, Sam's aggressive personality meant that they are subject to harsher criticism than their coworkers with more feminine gender expressions. "My more recent boss was way more of a hard ass with me largely because I think he had expectations of me to be able to take harsher communication . . . there's an assumption that I can be talked to like I'm another guy."

Sam's communication style caused clients at their advertising agency to assume that they were in charge, rather than their supervisor who presented more femininely. "There were a number of times I would be in meetings and . . . because of the way I was communicating if a vendor was coming in to pitch to us, there was often an assumption that I was more in charge." It is evident that Sam's success at work was attributed to their masculine expression. "They were like singing my praises and patting me on the back and the director made this snarky comment, 'We should get all of the women here to wear ties.'" Sam's physical and behavioral presentation afforded them access to the "boy's club" and shielded them from much of the gender discrimination their feminine coworkers experience, especially from a particularly misogynistic boss. "I did not end up [being] made so uncomfortable as I know some of my female counterparts [were] . . .

my understanding was there was something dismissive and sometimes outright offensive about what he would say. And when I interacted with him, he never messed with me." Access to the "boys club"
made Sam privy to the discriminatory beliefs many cisgender men
have against more feminine women in the workplace. "[This boss of
mine] had a very soft feminine voice . . . she was fierce and hard working and really competent and despite that, I remember hearing com-
mentary about how the way she communicates and speaks on the
phone, it's like, a 'How can you take her seriously?' kind of attitude."
Sam said he would try to "call it out and try to really diplomatically
and respectfully but still really directly [say] 'she's sharp and she's
competent and she shouldn't be judged that way.' " Despite Sam's
attempts to defend her, their ability to be effective in creating any real
change was limited, as they only got "pushback and some back and
forth about how the industry works and how you have to be a strong
communicator." Sam's masculine presentation allowed them to circumvent much of the typical gender discrimination women face in
the workplace, and granted them access to many of the benefits of
male privilege. "I would say I'm given a good amount—I mean there's
hiccups for sure but generally I'm given the same amount of prestige
and respect as other cis[gender] men." Sam's experiences reflect the
same idea that butch or masculine women are generally treated better
than feminine women, but also the idea that their place in the "boy's
club" is not always guaranteed.

Recall Parker, the white trans man in his twenties who worked as a
sales analyst and transitioned on the job. Before Parker transitioned,
however, he identified as a butch woman in the workplace. He notes
that as a butch woman, he was afforded more privileges compared to
more feminine women. "By identifying as butch in some ways people
expected me to be more aggressive. They expected me to be louder
and so I think in those kinds of ways there was room for me to be those
kinds of things . . . if I had ideas I was probably more heard than the
more femme women, who just tended to be quieter in meetings."
Parker's self-awareness has helped him feel compassion for the difficulties cisgender women face, particularly for those with more feminine gender expressions. "I was never a femme woman in the
workplace, so I can't necessarily say personally how that feels, but I
have to imagine it's very frustrating. There is this sort of sense that
you need to sort of dismantle your outward appearance in some way
before you can be taken seriously . . . you have to present yourself as
somehow not a threat nor a target, and then be able to get yourself
and your ideas out there just by themselves." Yet, these benefits came
at a cost to Parker. He had his butch gender expression challenged in

the workplace when one coworker told him to invest in a skirt. "[I remember] one coworker saying, well maybe I should invest in a skirt if I was going to go out somewhere, and especially in the Far East. I just wasn't going to do it and that really, I felt like it was going to hold me back because if everyone felt that way I wasn't going ... to travel."

As a butch woman, however, Parker faced the difficult task of balancing more masculine traits with more feminine ones. "Say if I walked into an office space, rather than people feeling at ease with more calm demeanors and calm body language and things, people would tend to be very regimented about what they asked and what they said ... it often took me being overly funny ... to break the ice to get people to calm down [so] we could have these more normal interactions when we're working together ... I felt I had to talk a lot and be open and make myself approachable so that people felt they could relate to me and we could talk more easily." Unfortunately, the taxing nature of this emotional work prevented him from engaging in activities that could have advanced his career, and his use of humor as a defense mechanism compromised his perceived competence. "Even though I got my tasks done, I took things so lightly that it appeared as though I didn't understand the gravity of the situation or of the task at hand ... I think it's easy to see or to interpret my interactions with a lot of things we did with disregard." While Parker was granted certain advantages in his workplace due to his more masculine interactional style, he had to take significant efforts to do the emotional labor needed to make sure others were comfortable with him. "If someone was apparently uncomfortable then I would try and be compensating by being funny ... so it makes it really hard to take myself seriously, or take my life seriously, when I'm making a joke of it, a mockery of it a lot of the time."

Parker didn't feel a part of the boys' club until after transitioning, but before transitioning wasn't exactly a part of the "girls' club" either. "There was this kind of men's space here and women's space here, I just wasn't necessarily welcome more or less to either place. So I would kind of sit somewhere in the middle ... and that was kind of othering in that way. So it was just kind of secret social space, I wasn't really allowed to bridge either." Parker's experiences while identifying as a butch woman speak to the tenuousness of the privilege butch women receive at work. While granted more agency and wiggle room to be assertive without incurring backlash effects, Parker nevertheless had to manage the little room they had to be "masculine but not so masculine as to be threatening" and "feminine, but only as little as possible to be seen as a woman." The difficulty of this endeavor can be inferred by Parker's relief at how easy it became one he transitioned at work and was seen as a trans man.

Recall Kai, the white transmasculine person in his thirties who worked primarily in Arizona as a veterinarian and transitioned on the job. Before transitioning, he was perceived as a butch woman in his workplace. At first, he was met with distrust and hostility, saying, "it was really, really uncomfortable the first two weeks I worked there. They had never had a presenting big old lesbian coming to the practice." However, Kai was able to earn respect from his coworkers by demonstrating his strong work ethic and taking steps to educate them about gay rights, eventually arriving at a place where he was his boss's "fill-in-the-blank person . . . his surgical gofer." Kai's brief workplace experiences as a butch woman show in particular the potential negative side effects of being butch: being perceived as a lesbian and mistreated accordingly. That this happened to Kai in Arizona (and not to anyone who worked in California) suggests that perhaps the homophobia of a given region will affect some of the negative associations with a butch identity.

Jordan, while identifying as agender, was almost universally perceived as a butch woman at every place of employment Jordan has worked at. Jordan's more masculine gender expression and interactional style were disadvantageous in the long run. When working as a realtor, Jordan's boss felt threatened by Jordan's appearance and the men's suits Jordan wore. "She really hated me . . . maybe it was how I presented . . . She really couldn't stand me . . . she screwed me over in a year review . . . I always felt like she was threatened by me. I threatened her in some way. Now that I look back, it probably was [my gender] expression." Jordan also quit a job as a long-term insurance agent because of another discriminatory boss, who verbally harassed Jordan. "She would call me up on the phone and tell me that she thought I should go to work at McDonalds." Jordan has experienced micromanaging from this boss as a result of not only work performance but for Jordan's nonconforming gender expression. This boss criticized the way Jordan dressed and often made comments saying that Jordan was not "feminine enough." Jordan believed that this unfair scrutiny was "very gender specific." Jordan's experiences reflect the potential dangers of identifying as butch and skewing too far masculine, and not enough feminine. The comprehensive and pervasive discrimination that Jordan experienced strongly suggest that there is an upper ceiling to the amount of masculinity a butch woman—or someone perceived to be one—can express and still be beneficial.

Cassidy, an Asian American transmasculine person in their twenties, worked in several workplaces while identifying as "butch." Although the way Cassidy has identified has changed, their physical presentation remained relatively constant. "My physical appearance didn't really change that much, my clothes, my mannerisms that didn't change . . . I latched on to wearing more traditional male clothes from a very early age, like bow ties, ties, [and] men shirts." Cassidy described how, as a butch woman, they had to exert a significant amount of effort to have their masculinity acknowledged and how that has changed with masculinizing HRT. "Being on testosterone has really let my maleness just come through as opposed to when I was a butch identified person, when I had to push for people to recognize me as something masculine."

When Cassidy worked as a microbiologist, they identified as a butch lesbian and had a masculine gender expression. As they exhibited more characteristically masculine behavior that matched with their masculine gender presentation, they were rewarded with a raise, "I asked for it. I demanded better . . . people took me seriously . . . I'm very competent at the things I do." At his next job, Cassidy worked as a biotech consultant and identified as trans but received feminine pronouns upon their own request. Cassidy, who worked in a male-dominated field, believed they benefited from male privilege and increased workplace respect as a result of the deepening of their voice and their general masculine gender expression. "I went to a leadership council and they put us in different groups of people and it was a female dominated space. Once again, every woman waited for me to speak before they would even speak . . . I sat there knowing my male privilege. I was completely aware of it. So I sat down and I waited for a woman to speak and they were all completely silent and . . . I purposely did not speak . . . Even though there was no leader who is chosen within this group, [they] would always look to me to confirm something or look to me, 'What do you think Cassidy?' and it's like I'm not in charge here, it's a group effort. But I felt that very strongly as a male masculine presence that I was in charge of things."

Although Cassidy experienced some male privilege in their interactions with women, they were also harassed for being gay. "One of the founders went up to me and she was like, 'Cassidy, I'm been meaning to ask you a question.' She asked, 'Why are you so gay?'" Cassidy's coworkers were also homophobic, and, as a result, Cassidy did not feel safe being open about their trans identity. "People were really mean to me as far as just being gay, just being gay alone and I think like being trans would have like blown their brains apart." When Cassidy identified as a butch woman, they had many of the same experiences as others interviewed—while on the one hand benefiting from a greater licensing to be assertive and greater perceived competence and authority compared to feminine cisgender women, Cassidy was nevertheless negatively affected by homophobic stereotypes in the workplace.

The Big Ideas

- Overwhelmingly, butch women were treated better than feminine women in every workplace. Butch women are able to dodge discrimination related to more "masculine" behaviors like asserting opinions, taking initiative, and voicing dissent, all behaviors that feminine women are typically sanctioned for undertaking. Butch women may receive more license to carry these masculine behaviors out due to them appearing in line with butch women's typically more masculine appearance and interactional style.
- While some butch women are welcomed into boy's clubs and men's circles, others are not. Some of the factors that may affect this variability include workplace culture and degree to which butch women are able to embody the "correct" balance of masculinity and femininity.
- Butch women who overperform masculinity are sanctioned for not being feminine enough, and lose many of the privileges that they may have received for being more masculine than feminine women. This may be because, past a certain degree of masculinity, butch women are perceived as threatening and unlikable.
- Butch women, and those perceived to be butch women, seem to evoke negative status beliefs related to lesbian identity in some people. As a result, whether or not the women themselves identify as lesbian, they are often the target of homophobic remarks and sentiments.

CONCLUSION

Examining the relationship between cisgender men and cisgender women leads to the conclusion that masculinity is a strong predictor of workplace treatment and outcomes: those who are masculine end up having a better experience in the workplace than those who are not. The experiences of gender-diverse people complicate this simple conclusion.

The experiences of the six trans women, all of whom transitioned away from hegemonic masculinity, demonstrate basic support for the theme that masculine is superior. Every one of them, with the exception of Leslie, noted that after transitioning they perceived themselves as having less privilege than they had before transitioning. However, these trans women were perceived in many different ways. All of the trans women reported being perceived as cross-dressers during some point of their transition process, if not still currently, and thus were viewed as highly deviant men displaying an intensely alternative masculinity. Other times, they were seen as women, and experienced discrimination on the basis of their femininity and ability to perform, specifically, cisgender femininity. Still other times they were seen as women, but as *trans women*—and accordingly faced trans status discrimination and unique stereotypes about trans women. If the worst experiences were reported by those who were seen as cross-dressing men, and the best experiences reported by those who were seen as the "right" kind of trans woman, then it cannot be said that masculinity is always and without exception better than femininity. For many of these trans woman, it was highly advantageous to be categorized as women, rather than men, in any scenario. We take note of this interesting observation for now, and move on.

The experiences of the four trans men interviewed add further complexity to the idea of hegemonic masculinity. To begin with, a legitimate masculinity was available only to those trans men who passed as men—usually requiring masculinizing HRT to do so. For those trans men who were able to pass, a hierarchy of masculinities was clearly observed in which trans men who were able to embody hegemonic masculinity (Parker) enjoyed privileges head and shoulders above those of men embodying subordinate or alternate masculinities (Kai and Blake). Trans men who embody hegemonic masculinity are inducted into the "boy's club," men's networks and circles where same-gender camaraderie—what sociologists would call "homosociality"—maintained exclusive workplace environments. Trans men who fail to live up to this standard are teased, mocked, disparaged, and delegitimized by others in the workplace for not being "man enough." To gain entrance to the highly selective ranks of hegemonic masculinity, a trans man must not only appear conventionally masculine—be sufficiently tall, have a sufficiently low voice, and display secondary sex characteristics like facial hair—but also *act* conventionally masculine in terms of speaking styles, clothing choices, and mannerisms. This is a high bar to meet, but also for many trans men is an inauthentic goal to strive for. There is accordingly a large range of possibilities in which trans men uniquely compromise between authenticity of gender and desired workplace treatment.

Finally, the stories from butch women (and those who at some point identified and worked as butch women) provide strong support for the mixed results in the research literature. Overall, every person who reported a workplace experience while working as a butch woman described how butch womanhood was valued over feminine womanhood in most ways, *if and only if* the butch women in question were able to keep their masculinity within a blurrily defined range. Butch women who were too masculine, like Jordan, are seen as threatening and lose many of the perks they receive due to their butch womanhood. Additionally, some interviewees spoke of negative experiences associated with presenting as a butch woman in homophobic environments, due to the associations of a butch gender presentation with a lesbian identity.

In general, is masculinity advantaged over femininity? Perhaps. From the stories of trans men and trans women, we saw that hegemonic masculinity was advantaged compared to subordinate masculinities, including "deviant masculinity"—frequently assigned to trans women perceived as cross-dressing men. Butch women faced an interesting paradox in which the more masculine they presented, the better they were treated in the workplace—yet, if they were seen as "too" masculine, they faced heavy social sanctioning. Trans women faced their own paradox: those who did not present in feminine ways were typically viewed as men, and sanctioned due to possessing a "subordinate masculinity," yet the most "hyper-feminine" of the trans women interviewed were likely to be read as cross-dressing men, and accordingly faced extreme discrimination.

How can we make sense of these patterns? One explanation may be that the far extremes of masculinity and femininity are safely accessible only by cisgender men and women, respectively. AFAB people have more license to access masculinity than AMAB people have to access femininity, due to the higher status of masculinity in society—for this reason, AFAB butch women are treated better than AFAB feminine women, while AMAB feminine men are treated worse than AMAB masculine men. However, AFAB people cannot safely access the extremes of masculinity unless they are perceived as cisgender men. This is why Parker's masculinity earned him privilege while Jordan's garnered death threats. We suspect that AMAB people cannot safely access the extremes of femininity unless they are perceived as cisgender woman, a difficult (but not impossible) feat for an AMAB person transitioning after adolescence. This was something none of the trans women interviewed for this book were able to achieve.

CHAPTER FIVE

Just Pick One!

One of the most common narratives explaining the trans experience is that trans people are "trapped in the wrong body." For decades, trans people have had to justify their desire to transition in order to convince cisgender therapists and physicians to authorize transition procedures. In 1967, Garfinkel outlined the "natural attitude" about gender, which states that genitals serve as the essential indicator of maleness and femaleness, and that these categories are mutually exclusive and invariant. These beliefs about gender persist today as the foundation of both everyday and scientific thinking. The World Professional Association for Transgender Health Standards of Care outlines the requirements for receiving medical care, which are founded upon these beliefs (Coleman et al. 2012). In particular, the trend for physicians and surgeons to require the Real Life Test, which forces individual to present as the "opposite" gender for a period of time before being eligible to receive transition procedures, perpetuates essentialized understandings of gender. This test requires a binary male-to-female or female-to-male transition experience in which gender identity, gender expression, and ultimately genitalia are seen as needing to be congruent to binary understandings of sex and gender as synonymous.

While the Real Life Test is no longer common practice, its legacy remains. This medical construction of the transgender experience has perpetuated the "the wrong-body discourse" as the chief rationale necessitating a gender transition, and trans people who do not at least pretend to adhere to this narrative are at risk of being denied access to medical transition procedures (Roen 2001). However, while this narrative rings true for some trans people, trans narratives as a whole are certainly more varied than this singular depiction. Many people who identify as trans men and trans women do not identify with the experience of being born in the wrong body, and self-identification as trans can occur at any point in one's life—not only from childhood or early adolescence. Furthermore, this narrative does not reflect the experiences of many gender-diverse people who do not identify as either men or women, viewing their gender to be either in between or outside of the gender binary. These people may identify as genderqueer, agender, genderless, gender-neutral, gender-anomalous, gender-variable, genderfluid, bigender, or Two-Spirit, among other identities. They may choose to gender-blend, creating an ambiguous gender expression, to have a fluid or fluctuating gender expression or to have a gender expression that intentionally violates gendered expectations.

What of these people, then? So far we have examined the experiences of trans men, trans women, and butch women, and compared these experiences to the existing research literature on gender and gender discrimination. However, we have not yet explored the research literature on gender that transcends or subverts the gender binary. We do that now.

BEYOND THE BINARY

People are more able to tolerate the notion that gender identity may not be fixed than they are the notion that gender identity is not dichotomous, as demonstrated by people with nonbinary gender identities (Connell 2009; Dozier 2005; Gagné and Tewksbury 1997, 1998). In other words, people are far more forgiving of someone they view as transitioning from man to woman or woman to man compared to someone who eschews those categories altogether. The more an individual is viewed as flaunting the gender binary, the more intolerance they are met with from wider society.

Why is it that people seem relatively more forgiving of binary gender transition? One reason people may be more likely to accept people who transition between binary gender identities than those who transition to nonbinary gender identities is that they see the latter as within people's control. The prevalence of the "wrong-body discourse" discussed above legitimizes a framing of gender transition as a necessary correction to a psychological error, rather than a willful and agentic decision. Discrimination against those with an uncontrollable social flaw, accordingly, is far less tolerated than discrimination against those who "choose" to embrace a stigmatized identity (Kricheli-Katz 2012, 2013; Rodin et al. 1989). In fact, some research has found that people who choose to embrace identities that are stigmatized often evoke feelings of anger and dislike from others (Dijker and Koomen 2003; Weiner 1995). In contrast, Weiner, Perry, and Magnusson (1988) find that when stigmas are viewed as uncontrollable, they elicit pity, sympathy, and judgments to help. If people are willing to accept the idea that trans men and trans women are trapped in the wrong body, then they may pity them and perhaps even offer sympathetic suggestions in an effort to help them achieve their desired gender presentation.

Studies of the workplace experiences of trans folks have found that coworkers actively try to categorize trans people into a traditional sex/gender schemas and exert pressure on them to inhibit gender transgressions (Connell 2009; Connell and Schilt 2007). In these instances, coworkers address challenges to their hegemonic gender beliefs by continuing to view trans people as lying within the gender binary. The more ambiguous or fluid a trans person's gender expression, the more difficult it will be for coworkers to fit them into the binary they are invested in maintaining. Robinson and Bennett define "deviance in the workplace" as "voluntary behavior that violates significant organizational norms" (1995: 556). When trans folks refuse to pick a gender identity or maintain a consistent gender expression, and instead intentionally choose to blend gender identities or oscillate between them, their gender expressions are viewed as especially voluntary and non-normative in the workplace. Therefore, nonbinary, genderfluid, and gender-nonconforming trans folks likely evoke greater feelings of threat, which leads to more severe discrimination and a greater chance of discrimination.

This literature is suggestive, but far less developed, compared to research literature on gender discrimination and status. What do the stories of the many nonbinary and genderfluid interviewees spoken to suggest? We examine the narratives of 13 nonbinary and/or genderfluid interviewees to document patterns in their discrimination experiences, in the hopes that these stories will support existing hunches and also challenge gaps in the research literature. We have split these 13 interviewees into two categories: assigned male at birth and assigned female at birth. We choose to categorize these participants by their assigned sex at birth not because we believe it to be an essential characteristic of difference, but because our findings support the idea that sex assignment at birth influenced how others have treated our participants.

ASSIGNED FEMALE AT BIRTH NONBINARY/GENDERFLUID

Phoenix is a 28-year-old white nonbinary person, who prefers the gender-neutral terms "this one or that one" as opposed to gender-neutral pronouns. Self-described as a "soft butch," Phoenix said, "I feel like I am strong and masculine but in a compassionate, soft, open way." Phoenix has never considered HRT and did not desire facial hair. Phoenix tended to wear button-down shirts, vests, slacks, ties, and men's shoes to work, and displayed masculine mannerisms

like taking up space and sitting with legs apart. Phoenix's verbal interactional style combined stereotypically masculine attributes, like interrupting and offering advice without being asked, with feminine
behaviors, including discussing emotions and engaging in caretaking.

Phoenix was one of the few interviewees who discussed little to no
discrimination experiences, in large part because Phoenix was self-
employed in food delivery. Even in food delivery, however, Phoenix
described benefits accruing from this one's appearance, mannerisms,
and verbal interactional style, especially compared to this one's more
feminine business partner. "I think I have a lot of privilege [because of]
my voice and my speed, and the body that matches it . . . My partner is
also a chef and she has a food business, and when we go someplace people look to me to answer the questions . . . [and] to make decisions about
stuff. I answer quickly and I answer loudly, so people want that . . . I will
tell people to do things, no problem whether it's my job or not to make
something happen. Ultimately, the result is generally good." Phoenix
was aware that this one's more feminine business partner is not treated
as well as Phoenix was, and attributes these differences to advantages
that butch people have over feminine people. "I am certainly offered
more well-paying jobs more regularly than [my feminine presenting
partner]. I think it's not just her presentation but also [differences in]
our approach . . . I'm also really forward in asking for my compensa-
tion." "I think that [feminine women] have a harder time getting away
with being in control and being feminine . . . when they do it they sound
more whiny. Our culture has taught me that."

It is interesting that Phoenix, despite not identifying as a butch
woman, had many experiences that mirror those of butch women we
interviewed, likely because Phoenix was perceived by others as a
butch woman. Phoenix explained, "People will say that I am a woman
. . . and if they didn't do that, I would love that. But I don't want to
change my appearance to make them do that." In a related way, while
Phoenix identifies as genderqueer and preferred that no gender pronouns be used, Phoenix does not feel like this preference was a realistic thing to signal, whether through gender expression or verbal
insistence. "I doubt [people] have the capacity to conceptualize a
gender-neutral offering. I think that people in our culture are so
attached to the gender binary . . . it's not really worth it for me to have
a conversation with them, I think it takes hand holding . . . if I were
gender ambiguous I think people would default to 'he.' I don't think
they'd use the gender-neutral pronoun. If they are going to pick one,
I would rather they pick 'she,' but I don't want them to pick either."

Phoenix's response were to let go of some of the importance that this
one places on gender pronouns. "I have seen all of the kind of shame

that comes around saying some of these pronouns incorrectly ... if people call me by the wrong gender I try not to hold too much anger, I assume the best intentions." As a result, Phoenix was often perceived as and treated as if this one was a butch woman. While this was not optimal for Phoenix, this was at the very least acceptable.

Casey, an indigenous nonbinary person in their twenties, noted that several factors can impact how they are gendered. When they bind their chest and don't shave, they're more likely to get "sir." But when they are with their women friends, they tend to be called "ma'am." Casey had been on HRT for almost a year and a half at the time of the interview, which helped them grow facial hair and increased their muscle mass. While their voice dropped slightly, Casey was dissatisfied with it. "I don't like the fact that my voice automatically places me as female. I would really prefer to have a little bit more of a choice." In terms of mannerisms, it was important to Casey that they blend aspects of masculinity and femininity in a way that felt genuine, rather than try to conform to other's explanations. "There was a while there when I was trying constantly to have male mannerisms because I was trying to seek that external validation from other people by conforming to that role and then I got to a point where I didn't really—it just wasn't me. I was just trying to play a role and it wasn't working."

Because the concept of a nonbinary gender is foreign to most people, Casey felt like there was a greater risk of alienating folks if they initially described their gender as neutral and instead took a different strategy of first identifying as a trans man. "In my experience in workplaces that I've been, people just have never even heard of transgender people sometimes and I feel this is a safe stepping stone. 'There are two genders, I identify as the other one.' Okay, people can usually get that. And then, [when] people seem like they're a little more amenable to talking to me more, I'll let them know that I'm actually more towards neutral and usually they're okay with that ... I don't come in guns blazing going, 'I'm a gender-neutral, non-binary and you need to refer to me [with the gender-neutral pronoun] ze.' I respect people who do that. That's fine. It's just I'm a very shy person and I usually just do the things that cause less strife." Casey's experience strongly supports the suggestions in the research that people are often more receptive to the concept of "transgender" if it is framed in terms of binary transition, rather than nonbinary identity.

Casey was unfazed when they don't end up having a chance to identify as genderqueer or be addressed by with gender-neutral pronouns, so long as they weren't seen as a woman. "For me, being seen as male is not upsetting. Being seen as female is upsetting." It is unsurprising that Casey said this, given their workplace experiences. As a veterinary technician, Casey went to work wearing androgynous scrubs and facial hair, yet was nevertheless misgendered with she/her pronouns regularly at work. Casey found this misgendering upsetting, and was frustrated that despite their efforts to present as gender-ambiguous, they nevertheless "come off as female more than anything else." Casey received tips on how to be more masculine from their female coworkers, including that they "should be more assertive." And, in a work review, Casey was told, "I was doing really good but I needed to take more initiative and be more assertive." It is important to note that despite getting suggestions for how to present as more masculine, Casey felt less pressure to perform hegemonic masculinity because femininity is acceptable for gay men. "Presenting as effeminate or feminine ... [is] socially acceptable for a gay man to do. So I feel sort of liberated in that sense." Finally, we note that while Casey was initially proud of their trans identity, discrimination quickly changed their outlook. "After I had my gender legally changed and after I had a set of references that consistently referred to me as 'he' rather than 'she' then I stopped [informing potential employers of my trans identity] ... It was a lack of need to explain and also just because I wanted to have an even playing field with other people. I don't wanna say, 'Hi, I'm this weird person.' I wanna just say, 'Here's my resume.' When you meet me in person you will see I'm weird but until then, please just look at my resume for its merits. And I just don't trust people not to at this point."

Casey's experiences seem to resemble more closely the experiences of nonpassing trans men like Brett, in that the discrimination they faced concerned not being perceived as sufficiently masculine and having their masculinity delegitimized, and Parker, in that they expressed strong desires to pass and be seen as a cisgender man. While Casey wanted to eventually make their nonbinary identity salient, it was clear that being categorized as anything but a woman—and therefore a man—took precedence.

Hayden, a white and Latinx nonbinary person in their twenties, did not identify with the term "genderqueer," explaining, "I think that implies an even split and I don't really feel female, and I guess it carries a certain privileged white kind of 'gender studies vibe' to it for me, since that's how I was introduced to it ... I mean, I see the place for the term and I think it's rad that other people self-identify that way, but right now I feel comfortable saying that I'm masculine of center." Hayden used "they" most of the time when referring to themselves but was fine with others using either masculine or neutral pronouns, saying, "It doesn't really matter." Hayden said strangers were often unsure of which gender pronouns to use, and they estimated that they get "male gender pronouns 40% of the time."

Hayden believed that how others perceive them depended in part on what they are wearing, their hairstyle, and which body parts others might see first. They noted that, "I do have smaller hands than most guys, so if . . . they see my hands immediately, I feel like they are more likely to use female gender pronouns with me." Hayden was also short, standing at around 5 feet, and so their height almost certainly impacted the way strangers read them. Three years prior to the interview, Hayden changed their name from a feminine name to Hayden. Hayden has been binding their chest for two years and did not have or wear facial hair. They went on hormone therapy for about six months, but decided to stop when they felt "pretty comfortable" with their appearance. Hayden didn't have interest in further masculinizing HRT or facial feminization surgery, saying, "I love my face [and would not masculinize it] . . . I'm pretty okay with how I look."

Hayden's decision to pursue self-employment and choose jobs where interpersonal interactions were low means that they were able to avoid discrimination. They explained, "I don't discriminate against myself. And whenever I've interacted with sex stores that want to carry my stuff . . . most of the time they're owned by a group of people who are very open-minded. So that's definitely, yeah, not a very discriminatory environment." Before they became self-employed, however, Hayden experienced discrimination while working at a restaurant. At this restaurant, Hayden's masculinity and gender expression were constantly delegitimized and mocked by their boss. Their boss would say things like "Oh, you can't carry that pot, let a real man do it. You can't move that, let a real guy do it" and "Oh, you're lucky that you're in back of the house and not in the front of the house." With these statements, Hayden's boss communicated that Hayden's masculinity was insufficient and that this insufficient masculinity was causing their manhood to be "false"—or the other way around. Furthermore, he insulted Hayden by implying that Hayden's appearance was unpalatable to customers. Hayden's experiences also resemble those of Brett and Casey, trans men who strove to have their masculinity legitimized but were to some extent unsuccessful, even though Hayden did not identify as a trans man.

Lee, a white "genderfluid" person in her thirties, identified as "genderfluid" and also used the terms "gender anomalous" and "gender variable" to describe her gender identity, saying, "There are parts of me that are female, there are parts of me that are male. The ratio of those switches at different times more on a presentational level." Lee didn't like the assumptions that accompany the term "genderqueer," saying, "I try and pick other terms other than genderqueer because genderqueer has developed its own particular meaning. It means people usually imagine a female born, male presenting, young, typically white, urban person who probably has a multicolored or spiky hair or multiple body piercings and maybe a few tattoos, who is kinda punky, who might want to go by a third gender pronoun, who wants to feel some distance from their original gender and who maybe isn't comfortable with their particular body. That whole set of assumptions don't apply to me." Lee had no preference between feminine or masculine pronouns, but did not wish to be referred to with gender-neutral ones, saying, "He or she is fine. I don't much go for the third gender pronouns . . . most of my life I spent as she. Mostly out of habit and momentum, I'm she to family, I'm she at work, I'm she on my ID and all my friends it's variable." We have chosen to refer to Lee solely with feminine pronouns for sake of clarity, rather than referring to Lee with both feminine and masculine pronouns.

Lee's presentation as exhibited in clothing, accessories, haircut, and facial hair was very masculine, but her body—most prominently her facial hair—often leads to others to perceive her as a "bearded woman." Lee had tried several methods for removing her naturally growing facial hair, but four years prior to the interview decided she was "just going to be a gender weirdo" and let her beard grow. Lee was read as both a man and a woman, with strangers addressing Lee as "sir" as opposed to "ma'am" about 55 percent of the time. According to Lee, "I get 'sir' when I'm seated, so they can't see that I'm short. I get 'sir' when I'm wearing bulky clothing [or] . . . when they approach me from the back, so they can't see my tits . . . if someone can see me full on, who knows what they're going to say."

While it wasn't Lee's intention to be gender ambiguous, Lee was inclined to give herself permission to authentically express herself despite this leading others to perceive her as ambiguous. "I'm aware that having tits that I don't try and smush and having a beard that I let grow and having short hair and wearing jeans and then shirts is ambiguous. But it's not like I'm doing that to be ambiguous. It's just what I like." According to Lee, she liked it when others react to her beard on a personal level. "[The beard] changes my interactions with people a lot and makes me more aware of other people and makes them more aware of me. I used to be much more of a reserved wallflower, hoping to disappear into the crowd, hoping not to be remembered, shy kind of person. I don't really have the option not to be remembered anymore. So I had to figure out how to work with that, which I think has actually been really good for me. Also it's just kind of fun to see who responds and how, and a lot of them are surprising so I get sort of amused. I've been collecting and writing up the beard stories."

While Lee explained that while she has always been on "kind of the gender neutral side of female," she only began experimenting with her appearance after college. Cutting her hair was an important catalyst for her future presentation changes. "It was a week after I cut my hair, it was the first time somebody asked me my pronouns and I was completely surprised by that. It was like—I didn't understand why they were asking me but I was totally surprised. So that was sort of a milestone. Then, from there, I don't know there wasn't any particular point but I just started dressing more masculine. Then three years ago, about almost four years ago, I decided to grow my beard out because I'd always been kind of curious of what that might be like . . . my beard started growing when I was 13 and I shaved, tweezed and blocked and did near chemical burn stuff to get rid of it."

She viewed her appearance as "a particularly unique experience . . . [because] it is so blatantly obvious that I'm not trying to pass for anything. That I have a beard and I have big tits and neither of them is a secret and I'm clearly not trying to hide either of them." Lee's appearance often led to harassment and aggression in public. "I had one guy call me an abomination. I had three like 20 something guys sort of yelling at me across the parking lot. I had one guy bellowing, 'That's disgusting, there's a bearded woman, that's disgusting.' " We were surprised to note, given this, that while Lee often received harassment from strangers on the street in response to her beard and gender-nonconforming expression, she received virtually no discrimination in her work as a teacher. "[I] went to my bosses and said, 'So I'm going to grow my beard back out. I've done this before and it wasn't a problem so that's what I'm doing, just so you know, and it doesn't mean I'm transitioning or changing anything else. I'm just growing my beard.' They were like, 'okay' . . . [Then] I told the students . . . 'Well my beard just grows there. I just let it grow. Some women have beards, some guys don't. So I happen to have a beard.' That's the last I heard of it."

Lee's experience was one of the most interesting to document because at first it challenged our assumptions about the workplace consequences of a gender expression that blatantly violated binary gender norms. As a result, we dove deeper into Lee's story to identify more clues to understand how she was able to avoid discrimination. The first thing we noticed was that Lee was not able to entirely avoid discrimination—the harassment she faced on the street, while terrible, was not unexpected to us. This suggests that something about her school environment contributed to Lee's experiences. Lee mentioned that her school has a trans policy, which we noted as a potential factor as well—yet, it still surprised us that Lee reported receiving no pushback whatsoever.

Then, we chose to look not as Lee's appearance, or organizational realities about the school, but instead about how Lee explained her beard to others. She described her beard—her most salient gender-nonconforming characteristic—as being something that grows naturally and on its own, and something she had no control over. And, as if anticipating follow-up questions, Lee explicitly denied any desire to transition or change other aspects of her gender expression, saying, "It doesn't mean I'm transitioning or changing anything else. I'm just growing my beard." By discursively framing a feature that threatens people's perceptions of the gender binary as unintentional and uncontrollable, she may have undermined these feelings of threat, and thus circumvented discrimination. This strategy, in fact, shares many similarities with the "born in the body" rhetoric we discussed at the beginning of the chapter. It redirects people's feelings of threat by disavowing Lee's potential agency in choosing ambiguity, and thus successfully steered Lee away from discrimination. If this is true, then Lee's story is a stunning and vivid point of support for the idea that only *intentional* gender deviance results in discrimination.

Jordan is a 56-year-old white agender person who used she/her pronouns until a year before the interview. According to Jordan, "I have absolutely no idea what it is to be female or a woman or what it is to be male or a man." Jordan also identified as "genderqueer," which was described as, "I don't have anything to do with binary [gender] . . . I don't understand why you would choose one, either of them, and limit yourself like that. I don't understand that." Strangers used "sir" about half the time, more often if addressing Jordan from behind and less often from the front or when speaking to Jordan on the phone.

Regardless of Jordan's desire to be seen as genderless, others still attempted to gender Jordan. "I think with my hair and the way I dress, people will see me more as masculine . . . apparently my face looks female. I don't see it that way." Jordan used to exert a lot more effort to police Jordan's own gender saying, "I spent my entire life trying to mimic what it was to be female and not doing a really good job. But I knew I was mimicking it . . . in my head I was thinking 'this is the way I'm supposed to be' or 'this is the way I'm supposed to talk.'" Jordan used to make an effort to walk in a more feminine way before, but "now I don't care about it anymore." Similarly, Jordan sat in a way that might be read as masculine, but again "that's not why I do it. I don't do it to appear that way. It's just what's comfortable for me." Jordan was a direct communicator, prone to interrupting and exhibiting assertiveness or aggressiveness—"I scare the shit out of a lot of people . . . with my aggression levels."

Jordan experienced a large amount of discrimination, across many different industries and places of employment. Jordan received the most discrimination while working as an electrician, a highly male-dominated industry, where Jordan received rape and death threats daily. Jordan believed the intention of these threats was to push Jordan out of the traditionally male-dominated industry, noting that Jordan made others uncomfortable. At another job at a real estate agency, Jordan was pushed to quit due to the harassment Jordan received from a transphobic boss. "She really hated me, the only thing I could think of was that I was gay . . . or maybe it was how I presented because I wore men's suits. She really couldn't stand me." At yet another job working as an insurance agent, Jordan's boss harassed Jordan, commenting that Jordan was not "feminine enough," along with a host of more baffling insults. Jordan explained, "She would call me up on the phone and tell me that she thought I should go to work at McDonalds."

Despite Jordan's genderless identity, coworkers who interacted with Jordan frequently gendered Jordan as a butch woman. Jordan's discrimination experiences almost certainly resulted from others around Jordan feeling threatened by Jordan's masculine gender expression, another example of the "masculine threshold" described in the previous chapter. This term refers to the idea that people perceived to be butch women accrue more advantages the more masculine they present themselves, but only up to a certain level. Past that level, they are viewed as threatening, and sanctioned accordingly. Jordan's experiences certainly support this trend.

Drew, a white transmasculine person in his twenties, leaned toward the masculine side of the gender spectrum. "I don't feel like completely down the middle in terms of the gender binary. I feel like I lean more toward the masculine side." Drew also identified as "gender-variant," saying "I feel like I'm on more of a continuum. I'll wake up one day and I'll want to dress more masculinely and I feel more of that energy, and then sometimes more feminine, and then sometimes it just switches during the day." Sometimes Drew felt both masculine and feminine at the same time and sometimes he felt neither. His experience of his gender shifted throughout the day, or depending on the company he was with. "It depends on whether or not I want to fit in with them. If I'm around a lot of very masculine cis[gender] men and I want to fit in with them, then I'll try to use their language and

I'll try harder to pass and to not say anything that's effeminate. It's less so if I'm around a group of cis[gender] women, I'll kind of be myself more." At the time of the interview, strangers referred to Drew as "sir" 80 percent of the time. Drew said, "I kind of try to blend in a lot. I only really correct people if I get to know them in regards to my pronouns."

At work, Drew dressed in men's clothing, often binded, and wore his hair short, but coworkers did not always respect his desire to be seen as masculine. Drew might have presented more feminine characteristics at work if he did not think the combination of masculinity and femininity would disorient people and result in discrimination. "I would wear [nail polish] more often if I didn't feel a bit strange in work situations because I'm wearing all men's dress clothing and then I feel like wearing nail polish and I feel like that might make my supervisor or boss uncomfortable or upset that it's not congruent, that it looks, I don't know, that it might throw customers for a loop or something." Drew made the arguments that combining masculinity and femininity is threatening, an argument that is well supported by other interviewees' experiences.

Though he was presenting almost aggressively hypermasculine at an OB/GYN office where he was an office assistant, Drew was still perceived and treated as a woman by his coworkers. "It seemed like no matter how much I tried to exert my masculine side and be read as something rather than a girl, it didn't work. Some of them tried to call me Drew and some of them just said, 'This is too confusing. Sorry we're not going to bother with that' . . . They'd still treat me as though I was one of the girls." Drew's experiences in the OB/GYN office may have been particularly discriminatory due to the highly gendered nature of the workplace, as well.

At his next job at a hardware store, Drew "had gotten up the courage to ask people [to use male pronouns when referring to him] and one guy said he didn't understand. It's like he couldn't separate my biological gender from the one that I wanted to be called. He said, 'I don't understand it but I'll try and if I shoot from the hip I'm probably going to say she. So don't be offended but that's what's going to happen.' " While working at another job in retail, a different coworker remarked, "I know that you are male but when I look at your face it just looks so round and feminine that I'm going to call you she." Drew's coworkers' unwillingness to acknowledge Drew's masculinity and refusal to use masculine pronouns was not only damaging to Drew's sense of self but also repeatedly caused awkward and potentially dangerous situations with customers. Drew, like the trans men and many of the AFAB nonbinary people interviewed, similarly prioritized passing as a cisgender man as a priority before his gender fluidity and nonbinary identity were even to be considered.

The Big Ideas

- In general, while every AFAB nonbinary and/or genderfluid person identified outside of the traditional man/woman gender binary, no one with the exception of Lee was able to be perceived or categorized as "genderqueer" or "gender-variant."
- Most AFAB nonbinary and/or genderfluid people interviewed were either perceived as butch women or as nonpassing trans men and evaluated accordingly, making the nonbinary identity effectively nonsalient for every interviewee.
- Most AFAB nonbinary and/or genderfluid people were satisfied with being perceived in this way, many of them noting that actually being seen as nonbinary was either impossible or too dangerous.
- Only one interviewee visibly challenged the gender binary, but the discrimination she received appeared to be mediated by her framing her gender-nonconformity as unintentional and biological, rather than an intentional choice to upset others.

ASSIGNED MALE AT BIRTH NONBINARY/GENDERFLUID

Jessie, a Latinx nonbinary person in their forties, described how they "lean toward genderqueer and andro[gynous] forms of expression." When asked what genderqueer means, Jessie said, "I think I definitely sense a combination of both [masculine and feminine] and I tend to identify most closely with some butch dykes, some tomboyish andro women in terms of not wanting to be male but nonetheless be somewhat masculine." When strangers interacted with Jessie, they used both "ma'am" and "sir" equally. With regard to pronoun preference, Jessie said, "Ideally I'd like to be not gendered at all, either way. Earlier on, maybe a few years ago, I would have just mostly preferred just only female pronouns. Right now, I usually just prefer that there wouldn't be any—that I wouldn't just be gendered at all, period." Although it is awkward in prose, we respect Jessie's wishes and do not use any pronouns when referring to Jessie.

Jessie decided to transition in 2000 and underwent electrolysis and four years of HRT, but has since drifted back toward androgyny. Jessie legally changed from a stereotypically masculine to feminine name, but now uses a more gender-ambiguous one. Jessie came to the Bay

Area from Montreal, Mexico, to begin transitioning because Jessie "
figured the Bay Area was the best place to be."

Jessie had concerns about safety and managed potential threats of
harassment by choosing to "not do anything that's likely to get people's attention, or at least [the attention of] that kind of people that
sometimes feel that they have to challenge people if they appear to
be gender nonconforming." Although Jessie would have liked to
express masculinity without being perceived as a cisgender man, Jessie's physique, standing 6 feet tall and weighing 250 pounds, limited
this ability. "Sometimes I just wish . . . I could be a lot butcher and get
by with short hair and what not. But obviously I realize that's really
not a very realistic possibility . . . because of the kind of build that
I have it'd be just really difficult. I mean I'm probably too tall and too
husky. I think that just tends to read a lot more masculine for most people." Even if Jessie could be read as nonbinary, Jessie identified that
this would be a dangerous place to be. Jessie argued that even cisgender people who are comfortable with trans people are tolerant only of
people with a binary identity and expression. "Because a lot of the
times even . . . cis people that are more or less comfortable with the
idea of some folks being trans . . . seem to think that if you don't look
stereotypically male or female that either you haven't worked at it
long enough or that you are not making as much of an effort as you
should be. They can accept that you have transitioned, but . . . expect
everybody to be binary-identified. It's kind of like binary reinforcement; they want to enforce the binary."

Jessie's gender presentation experience was in part governed by
the intersectionality of Jessie's racial and disabled identities. Jessie
shared that working in a Latinx culture impeded Jessie's ability to
be perceived as feminine due to Jessie's body size. "This was a Latino
environment and because most Latino women tend to be very petite
usually. I think that made it very difficult for them to see me as anything other than male." The way Jessie's autism was perceived by
others was also impacted by Jessie's gender presentation. The more
"heteronormative" and "inconspicuous" Jessie's presented, the easier it was for Jessie to cope with Jessie's autism. "Before transition . . .
just going through the world in a heteronormative fashion and just
looking like normal non-trans people do . . . if occasionally I spoke
out of turn or I missed some social cues, you still get a lot more leeway, like I said, if you have a little bit more privilege, which you do
if you present as a cis guy . . . But when you present in a way that
sometimes makes people uncomfortable just because of that, sometimes it can lead to people being a little more cruel or insensitive.
And that makes autism worse because sometimes it's hard to control

not to be very outraged or very shaken up . . . you get into unpleasant situations and sometimes you'll obsess about it or you won't be able to stop thinking about it for days or sometimes weeks and it kind of happened to me." Jessie decided to stop HRT in fear that it possibly "made it harder for me to handle my disability." Jessie's aggression, which was often related to Jessie's autism, was better received when Jessie was read as a man rather than a woman because then Jessie was perceived to be a "normal assertive guy."

While working at a Spanish language newspaper, Jessie's coworkers consistently used he/him pronouns for Jessie despite being asked otherwise by the HR department. As soon as Jessie began taking the initiative to correct coworkers, however, Jessie's supervisors tried to pressure Jessie to quit. "It was just pretty obvious that they no longer really felt comfortable with my being there . . . I would say that they tried to like pile as many things on me as possible just to see if I could just bear with it, handle it or what not. But there were obviously just looking for any excuse they could think of." In response to this discrimination, Jessie chose to rely on freelancing work so Jessie can control the type of clients Jessie sought out, usually from LGBT and Ally networks. Because of this, Jessie began experiencing much less discrimination.

Jessie's experiences place Jessie in a difficult situation: Jessie wanted neither to be seen as a man, nor to be seen as a feminine woman. However, because Jessie was AMAB, Jessie must perform a certain degree of disingenuous womanhood to receive she/her pronouns in much the same way that trans women interviewees discussed. Since Jessie did not perform this womanhood, Jessie was perceived often as a cisgender man—a more privileged but far less comfortable identity for Jessie. Jessie's ideal appearance—being perceived as a butch woman—was highly difficult to attain due to this situation. If Jessie presented butch, Jessie was seen to be a man. If Jessie wanted to be seen as a woman, Jessie could not appear butch. This Catch-22 makes Jessie's efforts at authenticity difficult to achieve.

Rowan, a white nonbinary person in their twenties, described their gender identity as "somewhat fluid . . . not explicitly female, but also not explicitly male. So varying, if you thought of it as a continuum, somewhere along the middle rather than at one of the two poles." Although Rowan wanted to be perceived as gender ambiguous, they were uncertain of how to make others unsure of their gender. "[Gender ambiguous] is how I wish to be perceived but I don't really know how to go about doing that super well. So I will present more at one side or the other because that's sort of how I know how to do it." Despite Rowan's identity residing in the middle of the gender binary, their presentation tended to oscillate to the tail ends. Rowan's presentation choices impacted how strangers read them, but overall Rowan estimates that strangers called them "sir" 80 percent of the time.

How Rowan presented was often contingent upon their environment, often feeling social pressure and choosing to cater to others' expectations. "[My gender experience] definitely changes too, day to day, maybe less, week to week more so depending on where I'm at . . . Parts of it depend on the kind of people that I am with, and then I feel more okay with being fluid. But when I am with certain people, I feel the need to try and be less fluid and be more consistent just from a point of view of meeting their expectations. The external change in how I present myself also somewhat affects how I view myself, if that makes sense." Rowan's ultimate desire was to be perceived as an ambiguous, nonbinary gender, but they did not wish to take hormones as a means of achieving this ambiguity. "Hormones kind of freak me out. They screw with your head and I mean that's the only part of me that I really care about working the most. All of the other things—it would be really cool if people couldn't read my gender easily, but I am not willing to risk that."

Rowan often received discrimination in response to their gender-nonconforming presentation while working for a mobile app company, and had their gender expression policed by their HR representative and the wife of their boss. They observed that on days when they presented in a more feminine way, with a padded bra, makeup, and skirt, they would receive much less respect, much more scrutiny, and much less friendliness from their coworkers. On days when they presented more neutrally masculine, this treatment reverted. Why would this be the case? It may be that when Rowan presented in a feminine way, especially given their aversion to transition procedures like HRT and surgery, Rowan was perceived as a cross-dressing man and as possessing a deviant masculinity. On days when Rowan presented more neutrally masculine, however, Rowan was likely perceived as a man with some subordinate masculinity, but not to the extent of a cross-dressing man. While Rowan desired to be seen as gender-ambiguous, they were aware that they could not achieve this with their current range of gender expression. That being said, Rowan valued other things more—their thought process being untouched by HRT and not upsetting other people, as examples.

Cory, a white nonbinary person in their twenties, said, "I don't have the words to describe my own gender reality . . . I'm a femme in butch clothes." Cory said that being genderqueer was "like carving out an outside space . . . it's like a 'both/and.' It could be male

and female but it's not necessarily. For me it fills all of those roles."
When strangers addressed Cory, they used "sir" and "ma'am" each
about half the time. After numerous and intense experiences with
trans-specific discrimination in the workplace, Cory wanted their
current coworkers to read them as a woman and use feminine pronouns because it felt safer. When Cory felt safe, however, like with
close friends and partners, they preferred gender-neutral pronouns.
For this reason, we have chosen to use gender-neutral pronouns
when referring to Cory.

A lack of respect for their gender-neutral pronoun preference was
the impetus for them to begin altering their body rather than just their
clothing presentation. "All the mentors and adults in my life [would
not use gender neutral pronouns] so I changed the way I was dressing
a little bit and they still weren't getting it, and it just became clear to
me that I was going to have to change my body instead of waiting
for them to change . . . It was a 'fuck you, I'm going to change my body
so I don't have to rely on your affirmation.'" Cory wondered if their
presentation has artificially leaned toward too much femininity rather
than functioning as a representation of their genderqueerness. "For the
first couple years, it was really about just affirming for me and being
able to see my queerness and have it be more tangible for me irrespec-
tive of how I was being treated in the world. But it took on this weird
spiral of chasing societally defined womanhood in a different way that
felt like a gross trap where it became a question of 'girl enough'
instead of 'me enough.'"

Cory had been taking hormones on and off for seven years at the
time of the interview and had a mix of secondary sex signifiers, including breasts and facial hair. For Cory, wearing facial hair was an act of
social defiance: "when I'm feeling . . . bitter about the world so then
I'm like, 'fuck you, I'm wearing my beard out!'" Cory sometimes contrasted articles of clothing with secondary sex characteristics to
achieve a gender-ambiguous presentation. "When my hair was longer
and I would sometimes bind my chest or wear double sports bras . . .
I still have a couple pairs of super boyish pants that sometimes I put
on but then I'll also put on a pushup bra." At the same time, Cory's
concerns for safety sometimes constrained their clothing options. For
example, "leggings as pants . . . I love how my body looks except I feel
my front is a little bit bulgier [*sic*] than most people's vulvas are and
the potential for violence in reaction to that is too intense for me."
When considering how they may present in the future, Cory said,
"I think that I'll probably be a genderific queer girl for the rest of my
life who's butchy aunt Cory that gets femmed up a lot of times and is
kind of queeny occasionally in a butch kind of way."

Cory experienced a large amount of discrimination throughout their work history in response to their gender-nonconforming expression. In order to decrease this discrimination, Cory opted to strategically modify their presentation in order to be perceived as a masculine woman, rather than as a feminine man. This strategy, along with their success in obtaining legal documents confirming a feminine identity, has allowed them to avoid much of the discrimination they were receiving.

Cory was one of the few interviewees who mentioned intentionally doing gender ambiguity and doing it successfully. What Cory found was that asking for gender-neutral pronouns was not enough; ambiguity was something they created for themselves by modifying their body through feminizing hormone replacement treatment. As a result, Cory gained the ability to present with multiple conflicting secondary sex characteristics, and add further confusing elements with their appearance and mannerisms. For example, while working in a kitchen, Cory got the chefs there to finally start using she/her pronouns for Cory by showing them her breasts. However, when Cory cut all of their hair off, this threw the chefs into confusion once more. At the time of the interview, Cory was significantly invested in passing as a cisgender woman out of a desire for safety and security after being fired multiple times due to their gender ambiguity. While Cory has the ability to appear gender-ambiguous, Cory felt somewhat constrained by their desire to be authentic and their desire to be safe, noting that the potential of presenting and being perceived as gender-ambiguous was not worth the negative hits to authenticity and safety. Their most recent experiences at the time of the interview seemed to reflect more generally the experiences of trans women discussed in an earlier chapter.

Rory, a Latinx nonbinary person in their twenties, was AMAB but identified as "intersex," saying, "I'm one of the many variations of intersex where the biochemistry doesn't align with the body which caused some issues. So I was assigned the gender of masculine and that's how I was raised and though most of my body fits that description, some of my body does not." Preferring gender-neutral pronouns, Rory also identifies as "genderqueer" and as "trans as in transcending gender but not transitioning to anything." They experienced fluidity with their gender and began experimenting with feminine presentations in childhood. When describing their gender experience, Rory said, "most of the time I feel equally both. There are some days I'll wake up and I'll feel very masculine . . . Other days I wake up and I feel very feminine and I express that energy. Most days I'm in the middle." Rory used to take care to present very ambiguously in effort to make others unsure of their gender. For example, they would "have half of my face in makeup ... if I was dressed more feminine I would let my facial hair grow out and also speak in a higher or lower register ... My voice would be one of the quickest or easiest ways to kind of try to change people's perspective of my gender ... or wearing makeup that was definitely not feminine makeup. I wouldn't try to look pretty." Rory says, "I don't consciously do those things anymore, I just wear whatever I feel like. I'm no longer trying to manifest what I want people to read me as through [my] looks ... I'm comfortable with my body today and I will behave exactly like I want to instead of try-ing to convince other people." Now, Rory intentionally works to main-tain a constant interaction style to avoid causing confusion for those around them. "In the past ... I would just let the shifts [between mas-culinity and femininity] happen and people become very confused. Now, I think I make a conscious effort to have more or less a baseline of how I interact with people to avoid confusion from the day to day."

Rory has faced severe workplace discrimination in every workplace they have worked in. When they worked in a mechanic shop, "cowork-ers would tease, 'Don't you think it's about time you stopped taking hor-mones?' assuming that I was transitioning to feminine." While working as an organizer, Rory was pressured to present in a more binary manner. "People assume that I'm not going to be relatable to people to the cis world. So it was like, 'Could you not present yourself as trans when you're speaking to these immigrant people?' For a time I would go with and it would be like, 'Alright, fine I'll put on my man cap.'" While work-ing at a phone bank, they were asked, "'What are you? What [do you] identify as? You're trans but are you transitioning to male [or] are you transitioning to female?' ... Once they tried to ask, 'Okay that's cool, but what were you born as?'" Finally, while working as a volunteer sub-stitute teacher, Rory was told that they had to conform more to a mascu-line gender presentation because they needed to "set the example" and that they "shouldn't confuse the kids." At the time of the interview, Rory was making a concentrated effort to find workplaces that are low in interaction with others to reduce discrimination. Most of their work experiences involved discrimination, and due to their desire to avoid conflict, they rarely addressed it. While Rory tried to avoid discrimina-tory situations, it was difficult for them to do so in work situations that weren't solo.

Rory's experiences are another interesting and rare example of suc-cessful gender ambiguity. To achieve this, Rory mixed and matched secondary sex characteristics, like voice pitch and facial hair, with aspects of gender expression, like clothing and makeup. Rory, however, ran into the same problem that Cory did—they encountered feelings of inauthenticity and discrimination within workplace environments. As a result, Rory began making less of a directed effort to manage others' perceptions of them through gender ambiguity, while also taking efforts to make their baseline gender expression more consistent so as not to confuse other people. While Cory was now spending less effort actively challenging others using their gender identity, they felt much more comfortable in the work they do.

Cameron, a 40-year-old white genderfluid person, said being genderfluid means that "my internal sense of gender is variable in that sometimes from day to day it has happened [and] on occasion that within the span of a day, I am aware of that my gender has shifted. And it's not a spectrum from male to female for me ... I tend to think of them as two variables and so some days that female variable will be larger significantly from the male variable, sometimes it'll be the male variable larger ... But I've also had agendered days." When asked about pronoun preference, Cameron said, "If I'm feeling female, that's when I prefer female pronouns and [if I'm] feeling male, I prefer male pronouns. I haven't been in a situation where I've been feeling both strongly enough ... I've also not felt agendered or neutral enough around people where I've asked to be addressed with a non-gendered pronoun." We do not use pronouns when referring generally to Cameron. However, when Cameron was specifically talking about feeling or presenting feminine or masculine, we use the appropriate gendered pronoun.

When Cameron presented masculine, strangers addressed him with "sir" all the time, and when presenting feminine, strangers addressed her with "ma'am" 75 percent of the time. Cameron did not undergo or contemplate any transitional procedures or HRT. For Cameron, transitioning meant becoming comfortable with the fluid nature of gender and having the flexibility to modify appearance accordingly. Although Cameron would have liked to be able to express femininity at work, they resigned to presenting exclusively masculine in order to safely maintain employment. Some days she felt she was "totally cross dressed" at work because she felt "high female" but was dressed in "male slacks and a male dress shirt." Sometimes she discreetly modified her workplace presentation to be more feminine, like putting "my hair in a ponytail holder that ... would match the color of my shirt." If she was feeling more feminine that day, Cameron would often go home and change directly after work into more feminine clothing, including skirts, dresses, women's shoes, and sometimes padded bras. Outside of work, Cameron's presentation was also mediated by "where it is socially more safe" to present as a woman.

Cameron faced discrimination when she presented in more feminine ways or when Cameron's genderfluid identity was made salient at recruitment fairs or job interviews. One interviewer even asked Cameron bluntly: "If I get you this cattle call job, can you present consistently over the course of assignment?" After repeated failed attempts to obtain employment, Cameron chose to present masculine and avoided mentioning gender identity in the next interview, and Cameron was hired. Cameron would have like to present fluidly in this workplace, but when Cameron tested the idea out on Cameron's supervisor, she told Cameron she thought it would be distracting. Cameron hoped that after working there longer, the subject can be raised again. Cameron, like many of the others interviewed, was in a bind where Cameron must choose between employment and authentic genderfluidity. At the time of the interview, Cameron seemed to have chosen employment over authenticity, but was hopeful that at some point in the future they could ideally have both.

The Big Ideas

- All of the AMAB nonbinary and/or genderfluid people interviewed described the trade-offs they experienced between embracing a more authentic gender expression and ensuring their material well-being, whether through employment or avoiding harassment.
- Additionally, all discussed the disconnect between the gender expressions that felt authentically "gender-ambiguous" to them and the gender expressions needed to be perceived as "gender-ambiguous" by others.
- The AMAB nonbinary and/or genderfluid people interviewed were perceived as a wide variety of genders, ranging from cisgender men to trans women to butch women.
- While not all of these interviewees were able to be perceived as gender-ambiguous, many were. These interviewees shared a few things in common: they were able to successfully mix secondary sex characteristics associated with different genders (like facial hair + high voice) and framed their gender ambiguity as intentional, and interestingly, all happened to identify as intersex.
- As a result of appearing gender-ambiguous through this "gender-fucking," interviewees received unique discrimination experiences like gender policing and pressure to present consistently, as well as more blatant harassment and insults in the workplace.
- These experiences were often negative enough to make continuous challenge for these interviewees unsustainable.

DOING AMBIGUITY

In Chapter One, we discussed West and Zimmerman's seminal concept of "doing gender," in which manhood and womanhood were framed as categories which people's membership in had to be earned. A person was not a man until they looked masculine, acted masculine, and embodied masculinity—if one did not do these things, then they failed to "do masculinity," and thus failed to "be a man." Doing gender as a concept has been reimagined in many ways since it made waves in the sociology of gender back in 1987, but in practically all of its reformulations, gender itself was understood as a binary system under which only men and women resided.

We wonder if, given our modern understanding of gender as far more than a simple binary of men and women, this classic concept can be reimagined once again. If there is a way to "do masculinity" and "do femininity," might there possibly be a way to "do nonbinary"? Our tentative answer is: yes. Many interviewees, in addition to describing and defining what their nonbinary and/or genderfluid identity meant to them, also described a rich list of ways in which they conveyed and performed this identity to others (it must be noted, however, that just as many interviewees discussed keeping their nonbinary or genderfluid identities private, and thus did not talk about conveying this identity to others). These types of performances deserve further investigation here.

Gender Blending

Many of the interviewees, not just those who identified as nonbinary and/or genderfluid, discussed wanting to be seen as ambiguous. Some mentioned gender blending, a form of gender expression created by melding masculine and feminine expressions together to form a gender-ambiguous—or androgynous—midpoint. Drew, a white transmasculine person in his twenties, explained that in order to be seen as ambiguous, he dresses more like a "hipster." "I've kind of been getting more into hipster fashion just because it seems more androgynous. It allows men to wear skinny jeans. Skinny jeans seem to be a common denominator but women will wear like looser tops with it. So it just seems to be like these tight pants, loose tops kind of a thing. So I feel like I'm able to present more ambiguously if I try to do that." Rowan, a white nonbinary person in their twenties, wore "a kilt and some small bits of makeup" and shaved their facial hair to be perceived as ambiguous, and also varied their gender expression from more masculine to more feminine on a regular basis. Whitney, a white trans woman in her twenties, when presenting androgynously for interviews, would wear her hair down, tighter clothing, and a blend of masculine and feminine clothing, as well as very light makeup. Jessie, a Latinx nonbinary person in their forties, presented androgynously by wearing "clothes that are usually not supposed to be specifically male or female. That means that I can buy stuff either on the men's or women's section in any store."

From these descriptions, genderblending seems to not only involve melding masculine and feminine elements, but crucially, doing so in a way that mutes the gendered-ness of each. Genderblending is thus about balancing and suppressing the gendered connotations people assign to clothing, mannerisms, and other forms of gender expressions so as to signal gender ambiguity.

Just as striking as this observation, however, was the reality that genderblending was rarely successful as a means to perform a nonbinary or genderfluid identity. Despite Drew's efforts to wear hipster fashion, he was invariably gendered as a woman more often than not, and sometimes as a poorly passing trans man. Rowan's inconsistent gender expression nevertheless resulted in them being consistently read as a cross-dressing or deviant man, and Whitney too was read as an unconfident man due to her ambiguous presentation. Jessie, finally, was read as a poorly passing trans woman. What these experiences show is that while genderblending often caused others to pause when trying to guess these interviewees' genders, this pause was always resolved by simply putting a modifier—like poorly passing, ignorant, cross-dressing, or unconfident—before the binary gender, rather than challenging the binary genders themselves.

A few interviewees, however, opted to perform their gender ambiguity in a different way from genderblending. Rory, a Latinx nonbinary person in their twenties, explained, "If I was dressed more feminine I would let my facial hair grow out and also speak in a higher or lower register and vice versa if I would be dressed in more traditional masculine clothing. My voice would be one of the quickest or easiest ways to kind of try to change people's perspective of my gender. Wearing makeup that was definitely not feminine makeup—I wouldn't try to look pretty. I would just wear makeup to wear it." Rory wanted others to be unsure of their gender. "[Gender ambiguity] is what I was coming to terms with in myself. I was coming to terms that I wasn't either [gender] so I wanted people to validate that piece of information." Cory, a white nonbinary person in their twenties, described how they took similar steps to perform gender ambiguity while younger. "I started having a beard and went through a phase where all my hair was all the same length and all that but I was wearing spaghetti straps." At the time of the interview, Cory occasionally performed gender ambiguity out of frustration. "When I'm feeling super lazy or bitter about the world then I'm like 'fuck you, I'm wearing my beard out.' "

Lee's experiences share some similarities with those of Rory's and Cory's, so we mention it here. Lee, a white "genderfluid" person in her thirties, decided while working at a private school to grow out their naturally growing facial hair rather than continue to aggressively remove it. "I'm just going to be a gender weirdo and rock that," she explained her thinking. Yet, Lee's ambiguity was almost a coincidental afterthought, and Lee notes that they doesn't hold gender ambiguity as a goal. "I'm aware that having tits that I don't try and smash and having a beard that I let grow and having short hair and wearing jeans and denim shirts is ambiguous. It's not like I'm doing that to be ambiguous. It's just what I like."

In these three experiences, interviewees described combining elements of masculinity and femininity, like with genderblending, but having these be heavily gendered elements to combine. All of them combined facial hair, a secondary sex characteristic that few would associate with those assigned female at birth, with a high voice or visibly large breasts, secondary sex characteristics that few would associate with those AMAB. Augmenting this ambiguity are more conflicting gender cues like hair length and makeup. As a result, all were able to successfully perform a nonbinary identity in a social world.

"Genderfuck" is the act of using highly transgressive gender expressions to intentionally subvert ("fuck with") traditional binary views of gender (Halberstam 2002; Monro 2007; Stryker 2011). Through the deliberate use of secondary sex characteristics, stereotypically gendered clothing, and other highly gendered physical and aesthetic characteristics, genderfucking creates a presentation imbued with conflicting gender cues. A person wearing a dress and makeup with a full beard is an example of genderfucking. Genderfuck is a politicized identity, serving as a visible critique of the gender binary and as an act of defiance against a heavily entrenched system of gendered norms (Bornstein 1994).

Genderfuckers do not include nonpassing trans women, who are often perceived as cross-dressing men, or nonpassing trans men, who are often perceived as butch women.. Both these groups face social sanctions for their gender expression: nonpassing trans women are punished for abandoning masculinity yet doing femininity inadequately, while nonpassing trans men are punished for forsaking femininity yet doing masculinity insufficiently. What sets these individuals apart from genderfuckers is intentionality: to genderfuck is to politically and intentionally highlight the socially fabricated nature of the gender binary, and to be successful, it must occupy a perceptual space in which it intentionally forces perceivers to acknowledge binary assumptions by taking liberally from both gendered extremes. Genderfucking is often treated with hostility and blatant discrimination as many cisgender men and women feel threatened by such blatant acts of gender defiance. Connell (2005) and Risman (1998) describe this threat as "gender vertigo," the dizzying experience of encountering gender in a way that results in a loss of stability and order provided by the gender system. Because genderfucking offers an intensely destabilizing experience as an experience of gender, it is often successful in signaling a nonbinary identity—as well as, in more a more sobering realm, putting the gender-diverse people who do it at heavy risk for violence and discrimination. It is no surprise that every gender-diverse person who expressed a "genderfuck" presentation eventually chose to veer away from this high-risk, low-reward form of gender expression—or, in Lee's case, reframe the gender-nonconformity as unintentional, and thus less threatening. The discrimination accompanied by these experiences of genderfuck made continued defiance unsustainable.

CONCLUSION

Despite an increase in trans visibility demonstrating the mutable and fluid nature of gender, most cisgender people nevertheless maintain a belief that gender is fundamentally fixed and binary. Gender-diverse people, especially those who visibly challenge the gender binary, face significant difficulties interacting within this gendered system. We found that many nonbinary individuals put in significant effort to perform a nonbinary gender identity through an ambiguous gender presentation, whether through gender-blending or genderfucking.

Nonbinary and genderfluid identities and expressions are often invalidated in workplace environments, and people performing these expressions are often pressured to "just pick one" constant and binary gender expression. Maintaining a fluid identity and expression or inhabiting a position in the middle or outside of the gender binary is not an option that most cisgender people consider as legitimate, and indeed many reacted to attempts at genderblending by simply trying harder to categorize interviewees as a binary gender, and pressure them to conform accordingly. This pressure tended to take the forms of gender policing, hostility, and discrimination.

Additionally, we found interesting patterns in the way gender policing played out for gender-diverse interviewees. Overall, cisgender men seem to take the gender expression of gender-ambiguous people they interact with at face value, while cisgender women are much more likely to exert pressure on gender-ambiguous people to conform their expression to the gender binary. Previous literature on gender policing has similarly claimed that cisgender men are more likely to police gender expression than are cisgender women (Kimmel 1994; Pascoe 2005). We speculate that efforts by cisgender men to police gender expression are primarily directed at those they perceive to be men in order to preserve the privileged status of hegemonic masculinity—and that when these efforts happen, they are more overtly confrontational and hostile. If a gender-ambiguous person is not receiving gender policing from men, we thus speculate that this is because cisgender men do not perceive them to be men themselves, and therefore not as potential threats to hegemonic masculinity. It may be that this research shows a much greater pattern of cisgender women policing gender-ambiguous people simply because there is no motivation for cisgender men to police individuals whom they do not perceive to be men.

"Doing ambiguity" was possible, but only for those who were able to "genderfuck," or present with highly gendered masculine and feminine accessories, mannerisms, and secondary sex characteristics at once. That even a brief ability to disrupt the gender binary was possible is not to be understated—the concept of doing ambiguity is one that pushes the existing sociology of literature into new frontiers. However, we must also acknowledge that doing ambiguity "successfully" came at a great personal and professional cost to those who did it, and that every gender-diverse interviewee who genderfucked did so only for a short period of time. While future exploration of this concept is needed, the costs associated with genderfucking may make this very exploration difficult.

Lastly, it is worth noting that just because "genderblending" did not succeed for the interviewees in these book, it is not unrealistic to imagine it succeeding for other people, in other places, and at other times. "Success" would require a genderblending presentation being able to signal a nonbinary identity—a requirement that may be in the process of being met, at least for some people in the San Francisco Bay Area. Lee, a white "genderfluid" person in her thirties, gave her definition of a quintessentially "genderqueer" person: "a female born, male presenting, young, typically white, urban person who probably has a multicolored or spiky hair or multiple body piercings and maybe a few tattoos, who is kinda punky." That this definition exists at all implies that an individual who performs in these ways will be read by Lee as genderqueer—and thus successfully perform a nonbinary identity. This line of thinking suggests that if a prototypical image of "nonbinary" or "genderqueer" grows salient enough in a given environment, or for enough people, then a nonbinary or genderqueer identity can be performed by emulating that prototypical image.

There may be another explanation. Cassidy, an Asian American transmasculine person in their twenties who grew up in Texas, described how Texan norms of gender presentation were black and white in terms of masculinity and femininity. "Texans don't understand that there is a gray area in gender presentation . . . constant questions I would have are like, 'what is it, is that a boy or girl?' " In Texas, Cassidy *was* able to successfully perform a nonbinary identity through genderblending because their appearance was something that could not be categorized anywhere within the acceptable ranges for masculinity or femininity. In the Bay Area, however, Cassidy's gender presentation wasn't questioned in the slightest—they would simply be perceived as a butch cisgender woman without a second thought. The genderblending gender presentation which had once been highly disruptive to the Texan gender binary was now commonplace and unordinary for a butch woman in the bay, and so Cassidy was categorized as such. This suggests that successful performance of a nonbinary identity—doing ambiguity—requires expressing gender outside of the acceptable ranges for both masculinity and femininity. Paradoxically, perhaps because San Francisco's progressive culture allows for a broader range of masculinity and femininity, it also makes it much harder to do ambiguity. This interpretation also lines up well with the success of genderfucking—it may be that genderfucking is among the only gender presentations remaining in the bay that resists categorization into binary categories, and thus is among the only way to successfully "do ambiguity." Under this interpretation, we might predict that as the range of acceptable masculinity and femininity expands—for example, as cisgender men begin wearing dresses and makeup, and cisgender women facial hair—genderfucking may itself lose its "genderfucking" connotations.

CHAPTER SIX

Strategies for Avoiding and Reducing Discrimination

While gender-diverse people in the San Francisco Bay Area are legally protected, discrimination persists in the workplace and often goes reported. The 2004 Fair Employment and Housing Act granted statewide protection to trans people, yet data collected in 2008 by the Transgender Law Center (2009) revealed only 15 percent of respondents who experienced discrimination filed a complaint, and only 30 percent were resolved favorably. These small percentages speak to the barriers trans people face in reporting discrimination and to the inability of these legal protections to adequately shield trans individuals from workplace discrimination. It is unsurprising, then, that the most recent and extensive national survey studying discrimination against trans people revealed a host of individual strategies to reduce workplace discrimination (James et al. 2016). A stunning statistic: 77 percent of respondents chose to hide their gender identity, quit their job, or otherwise take efforts to avoid discrimination.

This chapter discusses the strategies that gender-diverse interviewees employed in order to avoid or reduce workplace discrimination. We describe how gender-diverse individuals conceal their gender identities and modify their gender expression, intentionally engineer workplace interactions, engage with workplaces, and utilize organizational systems of support. We identify and explore the tensions that arise between acting in ways that lead to individual benefits versus benefits for transgender communities more broadly, as well as tensions between short-term versus long-term benefits. It is important to tease out the rarity with which strategies can successfully reduce discrimination on both axes, and identify the specific mechanisms that allow these strategies to achieve more far-reaching success.

TRANS WOMEN

Kelly, a white trans woman in her sixties, described the procedures she underwent throughout her transition, noting major milestones that mattered to her including hormones and surgeries. However, these procedures were never explicitly linked to discrimination—rather, they were described as if they were necessary steps in a natural progression of "passing" as a woman.

Alex, a white trans woman in her forties, described a similar laundry list of procedures and also worked with a coach that gave her advice on how to pass. "She said, 'Here's a list of things I ask trans women to do' ... The way that you talk but not just your pitch but the choice of words, inflection, somewhat the choice of your clothing ... The way that you walk, the way that you use your hand, the way that you sit ... She focused on voice but she [also] wanted you to successfully get through life." It is this idea, that gender expression should be modified to "successfully get through life," that adds intentionality to these behavior and mannerism changes that Alex underwent. While these were and ostensibly still are strategies Alex implemented in her day-to-day life, she tried other strategies before transitioning at her tech company. Within her tech company, Alex tried to subtly experiment with coming out by growing out her hair and nails. While this experience was negative for her, it also signaled that the workplace would not be a safe place to transition, and factored into her decision to quit.

Leslie, a white trans woman in her thirties, utilized her company's LGBT employee resource group before transitioning. This group helped Leslie look into her company's transition policies, which supported Leslie in coming out and pursuing her transition with the help of her company's policy. During her workplace transition, Leslie additionally took significant efforts to educate those around her to be non-discriminatory. "I pulled [a coworker who had missed my HR training and made a discriminatory comment] aside; I probably had the most one-on-one conversations with her, filling her in on things because of her not really getting it."

Taylor, a white trans woman in her thirties, expressed a high awareness of the intentional use of transition procedures to pass, and questioned whether doing so would feel authentic to her. "I've realized I want certain surgeries but I'm not trying to be something I'm not. A name is a name and I can change that and, my hormone therapy, that's just totally equaled me out and just made me feel better. But [modifying my] voice—what does it do for me? I mean, besides provide some passability?" Later, when Taylor experienced a string of discriminatory work experiences and was having trouble finding a job, she also intentionally sought out an LGBT-friendly workplace to minimize the discrimination she would receive. "Because I had to start over when I transitioned, I got a job at this queer hotel, an LGBT Hotel where I could be out and so forth . . . It was exactly what I needed. It was a sanctuary with a welcoming owner and a welcoming environment and everyone who came was gay, lesbian, trans." She found this job through the Trans Employment Program, a support service helping trans people find employment. "At that time, I was so new and so scared and transitioning, and this was one thing that was 'trans.' I was referred there from another like, from a trans guy and also the person that was running it at the time, was just an amazing person and he made me feel so safe."

Robin, a white trans woman in her fifties, was as critical of the idea of passing as Taylor but nonetheless described how she went about doing it. "I got better with the makeup . . . the more female clues to my gender I can give them the less they see me as a man . . . the higher up and the softer I get with my voice, the less misgendering I get." Like Leslie, Robin made herself into an educator in the workplace. "I'm finding out that in a lot of times, I'm often the very first transsexual [coworkers have] ever met face-to-face. And sometimes embarrassing questions get asked and all this. I still recognize, well that's kind of the mantle that you take on when you're going to be different. You're going to have to educate a bunch of people." By taking on the responsibility of being the first trans person her coworkers have interacted with, Robin used her identity as a teaching point to humanize trans people.

Whitney, a white trans woman in her twenties, described the same desire to succeed in the world as Alex did and linked this success to passing. "I don't pass as cis[gender], and because it's easier to live in the world where you're considered cisgender, I want to get facial feminization surgery and things along those lines to get closer." After fruitless attempts to secure employment in her old industry, Whitney relied on a local LGBT center for developing new skills that she hoped would make her more employable. "I'm taking a course at LGBT training center [in software engineering]. So they have like a little programming class and I have my own experience with it just doing it on my own throughout the years . . . Hopefully something comes out of it."

The Big Ideas

- The trans women in this book tended to modify their gender expression in the workplace to better pass as cisgender women. The motivation to conceal gender-diverse expressions may stem from an understanding that intense discrimination often results from being read as a nonpassing trans woman or, worse, as a cross-dressing man.

- Interviewees seemed to view gender-nonconformity and gender ambiguity, whether intentional or not, to be undesirable.
- Interviewees discussed a relatively consistent set of (expensive) procedures—including feminizing HRT, facial feminization surgery, and speech/vocal training—as being essential to not only passing, but to trans womanhood itself.
- Interviewees were at times torn between a strong pull to undergo more procedures (in order to reduce discrimination) and to stop where they felt comfortable (in order to feel authentic). Continuing experiences of discrimination seemed to bias individuals toward undergoing more procedures.
- When trans-related resources were available, especially concerning employment opportunities, trans women tended to express gratitude for their services and used them frequently.
- Some trans women interviewees, if out as trans in a given workplace, felt compelled to educate those around them as a service both to themselves and to the community.

TRANS MEN

In his very first job, Parker, a white trans man in his twenties, was perceived to be a butch woman in the workplace. However, Parker described how the allyship of a cisgender masculine friend protected him from discrimination and gave him opportunities he wouldn't have received otherwise. "Mike had always kind of included me in some ways ... When I was butch I think Mike had my back for a lot of it. He really gave me a lot of opportunities that I probably would have been passed over for." In his next job, however, no ally existed and Parker instead avoided bathrooms entirely out of concerns for safety. Parker also went out of his way to be funny in the workplace, to the point of damaging his professionality, in effort to make is coworkers feel more at ease. "It often took me being overly funny ... to break the ice to get people to calm down [so] we could have these more normal interactions when we're working together ... but even though I got my tasks done, I took things so lightly that it appeared as though I didn't understand the gravity of the situation or of the task at hand." Before he transitioned, he also took the effort to contact his supervisor and HR to work out the details of workplace transition and identify what resources he would be able to access. "I wasn't necessarily sure [my boss] was going to be very sensitive and he was great."

Kai's experience is interesting, given that his strategies to educate people might have actually increased the discrimination he received. Even though it repeatedly prevented him from obtaining a job as a hospice nurse in Arizona, Kai, a white transmasculine person in his thirties, refused to change his driver's license to say that he was a man because he "wanted to educate people . . . because people need to learn." Kai shared more about his motivations, saying, "[the discrimination] just made me frustrated. It made me sad. It was very disappointing. People were very, very, very disappointing. But it made me try harder to educate people." At his current job at a veterinary practice in the Bay Area, he is willing to answer any questions clients have about his gender identity and expression. "I've had full-on conversations . . . I think I've educated more people at this vet practice than I probably have since I started transitioning." Kai reports that folks in California are more willing to ask him questions and engage in conversations with him, making it easier for him to educate others. Kai was unique in that, apart from these experiences as an educator, he didn't mention a single intentional effort he made to reduce the discrimination he received.

One strategy Blake, a mixed trans man in his twenties, discussed was being intentional about his bathroom usage. "I was too scared [to use the men's bathroom]. There are definitely people there that I knew would not be okay if for some reason a lock didn't work and I got walked in on or I happen to be sitting and be noticed that I was peeing." Instead, Blake used women's bathrooms but only during low-traffic hours to minimize the chance that his trans status would be found out. "I tried to go in the middle of my shift, not during lunch, which you're not necessarily supposed to do. But because my supervisors liked me so much, they just let me go . . . You make up ways to get around when you're worried about getting hurt or you're so used to kind of dealing with being a secret." As Blake became more confident about his identity, he became more of an educator. "I'm an educator . . . if we were all stealth, where's the education?" To offset the discrimination that results from being out, however, Blake opted to use his network of friends to secure him employment opportunities. "A friend of mine helped me get the job and that's been pretty much the thing in all my jobs."

Brett, a white trans man in his twenties, only used one strategy to avoid discrimination and it was a largely successful one. "I don't know if I would have been as promoted [in my job as a teacher] if I was like, 'No, you need to call me this and it's against the law if you don't,' or if I was more like, 'I'm going to come to work, I'm going to start testosterone and I'm going to come to work with a mustache' . . . having not done that I think has afforded me to walk that fine line and to have just enough [cisgender] privilege." By allowing himself to be categorized by others without insisting on a given identity and being comfortable with how he was perceived, Brett managed to completely avoid discrimination.

Cassidy, an Asian American transmasculine person in their twenties, described a few strategies they used to avoid discrimination. They solved the uncomfortable issue of bathrooms by going home every time they needed to use it. "I worked close enough to home and . . . just went home on breaks." When they were transitioning in the workplace, they sought HR representatives out for help and guidance. "I told the HR manager that I was male, that I was a trans male, and I wanted to use the male restroom and all those kinds of stuff. And I was wondering about medical care, auto insurance, if I identify as male, what would that look like, [and she was] just really upfront and . . . she was cool." Finally, while Cassidy was in the process of transitioning, they made the decision to seek self-employed consulting work, rather than work full-time, to avoid discrimination. "I do not want people to see me during this transitional time. I don't want to face any discrimination, I don't want to have any problems and so I established my legal connections prior to being on testosterone or at least that I know that I was in friendly spaces with different firms, and so I'm working with two different firms right now [as an independent contractor] doing legal work."

Sawyer, a white trans man in his twenties, chose to ignore discrimination for fear that by addressing it he would make others uncomfortable. "[People] would make mistakes [in gendering me] and then I'm worried that they would feel uncomfortable about making a mistake because they would be worried about making me uncomfortable."

Drew, a white transmasculine person in his twenties, employed a number of strategies. First, his bathroom choice varied depending on how he appeared on any given day. "I would definitely have to measure out [if] I appear more masculine or feminine today just in terms of using the bathroom." Second, his go-to strategy, like that of Sawyer, was to not correct instances of misgendering. "Sometimes I'd let it slide just because I felt like a lot of the men there weren't really accessible . . . when [the men would] occasionally call me 'she,' I wouldn't correct them."

The Big Ideas

- There were few dominant patterns in the strategies that trans men used to avoid discrimination, though interviewees discussed a range of strategies like using humor, relying on allies, self-employment, becoming educators, and avoiding confrontation.
- The only common theme across these many stories was that many interviewees discussed suppressing their trans identities, not correcting others and going with the flow of how they were gendered at any given time.
- It is also worth noting that few of these interviewees experienced much discrimination at all, whether due to their passing as cisgender men or due to personal comfort with passing as cisgender women.
- Very few talked about modifying their gender expression, perhaps because trans men were able to pass as cisgender men far more easily and to a much greater extent than trans women were able to pass as cisgender women, and because many trans men were perceived to be butch women and didn't express a desire to pass as cisgender men.

BUTCH WOMEN

Neither Pat nor Sam described any intentional strategies they used to reduce discrimination, in large part because both reported having received next-to-no discrimination experiences to begin with.

ASSIGNED FEMALE AT BIRTH NONBINARY/GENDERFLUID PEOPLE

Casey, an indigenous nonbinary person in their twenties, initially wanted to be open about their gender identity when applying for jobs. "At that point, when I sent out a resume or anything else, I put 'I am a transgender person' . . . If I can't get a job as who I am, then I don't want a job here." However, after their first intense experience with discrimination, Casey decided not to disclose their gender identity, once they were able to obtain the sufficiently consistent legal documents and work reviews. "I wanted to have an even playing field with other people. I don't wanna say 'Hi I'm this weird person.' I wanna just say, 'Here's my resume. When you meet me in person you will see I'm weird but until then, please just look at my resume for its merits.' "

This change of heart reflects the dilemma many trans people face between authenticity and economic survival.

When Casey wanted to use the bathroom at work, they made sure to wait until no one was inside. "A lot of times I used the females' but sometimes I used the males'...Nobody did [harass me] because I always made sure to go when nobody else was there." Casey also learned not to get upset when people misgendered them. "I get called 'she' a lot and I don't really mind it that much. It used to upset me a lot more when I was first doing my transition because it was like, 'No. I'm not a she,' but I don't see it as an insult [anymore]. I just see it as people being slightly confused, going for one or the other." For their next job, Casey strategically chose to work at a university that has trans-friendly policies. "[Interviewers] at one point asked, 'So I see on your resume you prefer the name Casey. Is that the name you'd like to use while you're here?' And when I was given the tour after I was hired, they only showed me where the men's [facilities were]...the university has a very trans-positive policy which is why I applied there... It's a very nice place to work if you're queer."

Hayden, a white and Latinx nonbinary person in their twenties, used a number of strategies across their many jobs. The first was to choose to stay stealth due to concerns of safety. When they worked at a day worker center, they observed a trans worker experiencing discrimination. Hayden saw coworkers "mocking her, like calling [her]...a faggot...I worked there when I was really kind of starting to identify...during the end of it I was starting T. But I never fully came out to any of my co-workers just because I felt kind of uncomfortable about it because I saw the way that some of the workers had responded to this one trans woman." The second major strategy was to seek alternatives to traditional work. They managed to get an under-the-table job through connections to avoid hiring discrimination, and dodged discrimination by finding work making and selling crafts.

Phoenix, a 28-year-old white nonbinary person, chose a strategy of ignoring misgendering. "I have seen all of the kind of shame that comes around saying some of these pronouns incorrectly...if people call me by the wrong gender I try not to hold too much anger, I assume the best intentions."

Lee, a white "genderfluid" person in her thirties, described intentionally modifying her gender expression in order to be hired as a part-time teacher. "I decided to shave my beard before the interview. I presented a little more female than usual...going for [a] butch... professional lesbian kind of look." Lee later decided to grow out her beard in order to feel more authentic with her gender expression at work and she did not receive any resistance when she discussed her decision with her supervisor and students due to the nonthreatening way she framed it. "It's not like I'm doing that to be ambiguous ... [I] went to my bosses and said, 'So I'm going to grow my beard back out. I've done this before and it wasn't a problem so that's what I'm doing, just so you know, and it doesn't mean I'm transitioning or changing anything else. I'm just growing my beard.' They were like, 'okay' ... [Then] I told the students ... and they're like, 'Wait, how do you grow it and how long is it going to get?' That's the last I heard of it."

Jordan, a 56-year-old white agender person, made no mention of any attempts to shape Jordan's discrimination experiences despite facing extreme amounts of discrimination. Perhaps, like Kai, Jordan was committed to living life the way Jordan wanted and was unfazed by any consequence received.

The Big Ideas

- The most common strategy for AFAB nonbinary or genderfluid people was to ignore misgendering—for many these people, misgendering was also one of the only forms of discrimination they received.
- Other strategies used included hiding a trans identity, intentionally suppressing gender-nonconformity, working in trans-friendly workplaces, and avoiding interaction with others.
- Lee's was one of the only strategies that involved interacting with others and, as documented earlier, succeeded in avoiding discrimination by framing a gender-nonconforming presentation as out of her control, and thus not willful deviance.

ASSIGNED MALE AT BIRTH NONBINARY/GENDERFLUID PEOPLE

Jessie, a Latinx nonbinary person in their forties, was forced out of a job at a Spanish newspaper when they started correcting their coworker's pronoun usage and had to rethink the risk surrounding that strategy and whether it was worth it for them. "Sometimes I just don't feel like going through that again." Jessie never filed a complaint about the discrimination they faced, a move that was highly intentional. "I didn't think it was worth it and at that time I was kind of concerned about possible consequences elsewhere ... sometimes if you file a complaint with one employer, sometimes all the people in the same field or the same industry—they can hear about it."

Due to this discrimination, Jessie worked to avoid being put into a similar situation again. "It became so traumatic for me to deal with [discrimination] and because I was just so scared . . . that I would get a job and that somehow something would slip up . . . there was still a potential that something I would do would get me in trouble and either get me fired." One strategy they pursued was working jobs in which face-to-face communication was unnecessary. "Sometimes I've done stuff just from online and just via email or text or whatever. So that's one of the other things that's been appealing to me." Another strategy was freelancing, which allowed them to control what clients they took. "I just wanted to just avoid like normal like nine to five employment and try to just freelance mostly as much as I could . . . Sometimes it's a little easier in the sense at least that you can control your schedule and try to figure out what kind of clients are going to be easier to work with. Occasionally if you have a client that you don't think that things are going too great communication-wise, you can just end the relationship . . . usually I'm either around LGBT circles or folks who are friendly to LGBT people. It usually tends not to be too bad."

Rowan, a white nonbinary person in their twenties, sought to resolve conflict without confrontation, which often looked like Rowan not addressing discrimination when it occurred. With pronouns, Rowan rarely corrected others out of a fear that it would create an uncomfortable situation. "It's not important enough to bother bringing it up and it sounds really awkward in a lot of places. I don't want to force people." After receiving intense pressure to regulate their gender expression while working at a tech company, Rowan decided to quit without filing a complaint, though noted that this was for professional reasons as well. "Tech is a pretty small community and I felt that if I complained about it like that wouldn't be good for the future. I definitely know I am going to work with some of those people again; there are some of them that I would want to work with again maybe at different jobs. I felt like if I complained about that they would have a not great view of me . . . I figured it would get me labeled as someone who was unreasonably demanding about such things."

Rowan was accosted in the bathroom at their next tech job. A fellow employee whom they did not know assertively said to them, "You are in the wrong place. You need to leave." After that experience, Rowan made sure to avoid the men's bathrooms at work. "I don't know, maybe I should have filed a complaint. I talked this over with a friend and they said I probably should have. At the time I was just like, 'okay, staying away from there.' "

Cory, a white nonbinary person in their twenties, was acutely aware of which kinds of gender expressions led to the most workplace discrimination. "I feel like I get treated worse when I'm identified or seen as the femme boy versus the tough or masculine girl." Having experimented with many different types of gender expressions, over time they concluded, "trying to pull off femme woman as an employed person got me fired for being a man with boobs and trying to pull off femme drag butch girl is working, 'she' and 'her' is safest for me . . . it's the best compromise between what would feel the best to put on versus how will I react to how I'm treated." Cory acknowledged that "the hyper femininity [they] tactically employ for food service work" was a strategic decision. Cory also identified the interplay between binary gender expressions, which may reduce harm and discrimination, and the effect that maintaining these inauthentic gender expressions has on both the self and the community. Cory was nevertheless happy with their compromise: "I think that I'll probably be a genderific queer girl for the rest of my life, who's like butchy aunt Cory that gets femmed up a lot of times and is kind of queeny occasionally and like in a butch kind of way." By embracing tactical femininity for work and more fluid expressions of gender in other situations, Cory created a unique strategy that feels sustainable.

In the workplace, Cory's bathroom usage was strategic as well. "It depends on variables, so how I'm presenting. I cruise for path of least resistance rather than path of most identification." Similarly, Cory's job in food service meant that they had to utilize strategies that privilege the customer interaction over their own comfort. "I'll correct people in terms of where I work . . . frequently when people will 'he/ him' me. It will feel like a slight on me. I wear a push up bra, I wear makeup, I dress femme-y. It's like, 'fuck you, I'm putting the effort and like let's go, pick up the cues and let's play.' But at the same time, I'm at their disposal as the server in the situation so I'll be like, 'he/ him, she/ her, either way,' and I'll say some kind of 'ha-ha' that puts them on point that that's not an accurate read." Eventually, however, the biggest boon to being perceived as a woman in the workplace for Cory was changing their identification documents. "The male owner [of the restaurant], once he gets one thing in his head, he's with it. So he's the administrator, he's seen that my ID says female. He's seen that my legal name [is feminine]. So I feel some amount of having that as a shield."

Rory, a Latinx nonbinary person in their twenties, employed strategies that were largely dictated by their discrimination experiences. While working in a school, a discrimination experience related to bathroom usage made Rory decide to no longer use the school's gendered bathrooms. "The daytime vice principal had me do a report under the guise of consulting about their legal ground to deny access for a trans woman to use the restroom at the school. Before I was given this task, I would use whichever restroom was the closest. [Afterward] I was going to the restroom a lot less often. They did have one single stall restroom for the faculty, which was often locked. If it was open then I could use it, if it was locked then I couldn't." Rory secured their next job only with the help of a friend who worked as a manager at a phone bank. While utilizing this strategy helped Rory get a job, it didn't necessarily mitigate the discrimination they received. Eventually, continued discrimination experiences drove Rory into self-employment doing bike repair. "Getting paid $300 to put a bike together is pretty sweet because like I have fun with it, right? It's also something I get to do alone after I get the bid; it's well, it doesn't matter that I'm trans, it doesn't matter that I present in any way. I could be doing the work in a skirt or I could be doing the work naked."

For Cameron, a 40-year-old white genderfluid person, strategies revolved around obtaining and retaining employment. While Cameron was initially much more out about being genderfluid in job interviews, joblessness became an increasingly bigger problem. "I needed to find a job and . . . now I've been either asked to be or have chosen to be limited in my presentation in my job." Cameron relented, saying, "as far as presentation, I toned down. I decided to present more male just because I thought maybe it would be the safer thing to do. Maybe make it more likely for me to get hired or at least for somebody to find me an assignment." Cameron acknowledged that the situation was unsustainable, and was in the process of trying to decide when and how to come out at work. Cameron was open to making compromises in modifying their gender expression for the comfort of others. "I would be able to say, 'Look, I'm not trying to disrupt the workplace here, however, my sense of identity and sense of well-being is directly related to my ability to present according to my gender identity.' I would be willing to negotiate with her and say, 'Okay, let's talk about . . . this week I'll present female consistently if that's sort of the benchmark [and next] week I'll present consistently male and then work things out from there . . . Satisfy me: no; within the bounds of what I believe is possible to achieve: yes."

The Big Ideas

- Overwhelmingly, the strategies used by AMAB nonbinary and/or genderfluid people were chosen in response to a traumatic discrimination experience.

- The most common strategy was avoiding the context, environment, or even type of work where the traumatic discrimination experience occurred. To do this, AMAB nonbinary and/or genderfluid people quit their jobs, stopped correcting misgendering, abstained from bathroom usage, and chose self-employment.
- Another common strategy was suppressing a nonbinary or gender-fluid identity in the workplace and attempting to pass as cisgender men. This was a strategy that was not without its psychological and emotional costs.

PUTTING IT ALL TOGETHER

Looking at all of the interviewees' experiences, we can see that strategies chosen to avoid and reduce discrimination were many and diverse. To end this chapter, we organize these strategies into similar categorizes, and also analyze each type of strategy according to its impact on individuals who implemented them over the short- and long-term, as well as its impact on broader trans communities.

Making Trans Invisible

By and large, the most common strategy gender-diverse interviewees described to avoid and reduce discrimination was to make their trans identity invisible. Some interviewees delayed their gender transitions, while other interviewees abstained from gender transitions entirely. Some kept their gender-diverse identities private from their workplaces to pass as the genders they were assigned at birth, while others transitioned and they withheld information about their previously gender identities. One common thread underlying these strategies was the shared belief that "trans was a negative trait in the workplace" and that hiding indicators of a trans status would thus improve workplace experiences, improve hireability, reduce discrimination, and protect oneself from violence and harassment. Another common thread was that all forms of this strategy relied on passing.

Passing

The concept of passing refers to the idea of managing identities (Garfinkel 1967). In the context of trans experiences, passing is a designation describing the act of being perceived as a certain gender identity, dependent on an individual's gender expression. An individual who passes as a man, for example, is perceived by others to be a man on the basis of external gendered cues like clothing, voice, and mannerisms. Passing privilege refers to the advantages conferred on those who are able to pass as a binary gender, that is people who are perceived as cisgender. Therefore, passing privilege can exist not only when an individual passes "successfully" as the gender they identify as, but also when an individual passes as the gender they were assigned at birth. Passing may offer advantages ranging from employability to safety, as individuals who pass as cisgender tend to experience less discrimination and harassment.

Some people, especially AFAB individuals made their trans identities invisible but made no efforts to pass. These individuals simply allowed themselves to be categorized, perceived, and gendered by those around them regardless of how accurate the perceptions were. As a result, these people moved fluidly through being perceived as butch women and as feminine men, regardless of their actual gender identities.

Testing the Waters

When gender-diverse interviewees were considering changing their identity or presentation in the workplace, often times they tested the waters to attempt to predict what the experience of coming out would be like. Some made small adjustments to their interactional style, physical presentation, or mannerisms to evaluate the safety of expressing various forms of gender-nonconformity in a given workplace, rather than jumping into an unknown situation headfirst. Others approached their HR departments, supervisors, or other knowledgeable experts in the workplace to explore their options. Information gathered from these trial runs often signaled to interviewees that a workplace was safe or unsafe. If unsafe, knowing this information early gave them opportunities to look for new jobs that would be more inclusive without necessarily threatening their old positions.

Ignore Misgendering

One strategy that many gender-diverse people employed to avoid or reduce discrimination is ignoring misgendering when it occurs. While many participants felt distressed when coworkers or clients used incorrect names or pronouns, many nevertheless avoided acknowledging acts of misgendering. They feared that correcting misgendering would negatively affect workplace treatment, their relationships with others in the workplace, or add to the undue stress of needing to explain and defend their identities. Directly addressing misgendering was often a strategy that placed a large amount of attention on gender-diverse people and makes their nonconformity especially salient. Therefore, correcting misgendering may make a gender-diverse person a greater target for discrimination, especially in workplaces that are not especially trans-friendly.

Many interviewees were aware of the trade-off between safety and authenticity regarding misgendering. Participants in this book who decided not to confront misgendering rationalized their choices in a number of ways. Some cited a fear of increased discrimination, some indicated that misgendering was inevitable and correcting it was a waste of time, and some stated they wanted to avoid making others uncomfortable by correcting misgendering. Though confronting misgendering has a positive impact for the larger trans community by introducing others to trans identities and expressions, this strategy was often deemed to be too uncomfortable or risky for the individual, especially in noninclusive workplaces.

The Costs of Hiding

When people feel forced to work a job where they cannot authentically perform their gender expression to validate their gender identity, they may feel emotional distress that significantly impairs their work productivity. In fact, a recent national study on trans discrimination found that "the vast majority (78%) of those who transitioned from one gender to the other reported that they felt more comfortable at work and their job performance improved, despite high levels of mistreatment" (Grant et al. 2011: 3).

As we discussed in Chapter Five, several gender-diverse individuals concluded that their workplaces would discriminate against them if they transitioned genders and so they chose to delay transitioning or suppress their trans identities. Others chose to wait until they established themselves in the workplace and earned the trust of their coworkers before transitioning. While these participants indicated that delaying their transition was a useful discrimination-reduction strategy in the short term, all acknowledged that it was an unsustainable long-term strategy due to the mental and emotional costs of being unable to authentically express themselves.

Being perceived as a gender-conforming man or woman results in better workplace treatment compared to being perceived as gender-diverse. In response to discrimination and negative treatment in the workplace, many gender-diverse people chose to conceal their identity or modify their expression even after they began their transition process in order to be more gender-normative. Many trans individuals modified their gender expression in order to preemptively avoid or minimize discrimination. Others reported being pressured by employers and coworkers to make changes to their gender presentation in the workplace. Concealing gender identity or modifying gender presentation at work is particularly successful in reducing negative workplace treatment if it enables an individual to pass as cisgender.

This strategy has a range of effects on the individual; it is especially helpful for trans women and trans men who view these modifications as a part of their transition process and are motivated to make substantial efforts to pass as cisgender for personal and/or professional reasons. For nonbinary and genderfluid individuals, concealing identities or modifying expressions to pass as gender-normative often feels disingenuous and is therefore quite costly, especially if this inauthenticity must be maintained over a long period of time. For these reasons, this strategy often results in both short- and long-term benefits for trans women and trans men, but tends to only provide short-term benefits for nonbinary or genderfluid people.

Concealing gender identity or modifying gender expression in order to pass as more gender-normative may reinforce the idea in the workplace that trans people should look and act a certain way to gain legitimacy. This strategy thus negatively affects the larger trans community by continually privileging a certain way of "looking" or "acting" trans over others, favoring those who seek a binary transition and failing to normalize gender ambiguity. While these strategies may be beneficial for specific individuals, they do not benefit the greater trans community because they diminish the visibility of gender-nonconformity in the workplace. Visibility in the workplace is important for gender-diverse people because it challenges binary assumptions about gender and provides familiarity with various gender-diverse identities and expressions. Each gender-diverse person who is visible in the workplace sets a precedent so that future gender-diverse people become progressively less novel.

Strategies to avoid and reduce discrimination by concealing gender identity or modifying gender expression were commonly described by trans women and nonbinary or genderfluid people, and it is important to acknowledge that this strategy was not mentioned by the trans men and masculine women I interviewed. Because most of the trans men in this book pass as cisgender, they have little need to strategize about ways to conceal their identity or modify their presentation to appear more normative—they are perceived to be and treated as cisgender men. Masculine or butch women are usually not perceived as adversely gender non-normative. Since they still identify as cisgender women, they have no need to conceal their gender identity, and because masculinity is typically viewed as superior, their masculine gender expression is advantageous.

Most interviewees struggled with resolving their desires for authenticity in gender identity and expression with the prejudice and discrimination that often resulted. Several participants described themselves as initially expressing an authentic gender identity and expression in the workplace, but later choosing to hide their identities or modify their presentation in response to continued harassment and discrimination. This creates a situation where the most positive strategy for the individual is often a highly undesirable strategy for the trans community, and vice versa. By hiding trans identity and modifying gender expressions in a way that makes gender-nonconformity invisible, workplace environments grow no more inclusive or trans-friendly. Additionally, this lack of visibility contributes to a larger lack of understanding regarding nonbinary and genderfluid identities. Many gender-diverse individuals decide that workplace safety, job security, and employment are more important to them than advocating for the trans community through visibility politics

Advocates and Jokers

On the other side of making trans invisible were those who made trans very visible, whether through more serious efforts like teaching and advocating or through more casual efforts like humor.

Educate Others

Education is a major theme in many participants' efforts to reduce discrimination in the workplace. Taking on the responsibility of educating others often placed additional burdens on gender-diverse people, and at times led to more discrimination experiences in the short term. However, every interviewee who took part in educating coworkers or clients described the pride they felt from their efforts to educate others. They believed that their efforts were creating change that would lead to reductions in discrimination for themselves and for the wider community. Educating others about trans identity was a strategy that was highly beneficial for the trans community, though individual benefits varied.

While efforts to educate others often place more attention on gender-diverse people that sometimes result in more discrimination in the short term, interviewees who relied on this strategy felt like they were taking concrete action to reduce the discrimination in the long run and would positively impact the trans community as a whole.

Use Humor

Another strategy many gender-diverse people employ to reduce discrimination is using humor in interpersonal interactions in order to defuse tension, avoid conflict, and reduce the threat they pose to other's comfort. Goffman (1963) and more recently Yoshino (2006) refer to the process of toning down a stigmatized identity as "covering." This covering behavior may result in modification of behavior in ways that unintentionally results in further disadvantage.

Many gender-diverse people use humor to try to deflect harassment. Others use humor as a tool for dealing with instances of gender policing. Though humor may have been effective in the short term in many cases, humor was unable to fundamentally address the tensions and prejudices within the workplace over the long term. This strategy for deflecting negative workplace treatment was largely unable to result in long-term benefits for the individual because it did not directly address harassment. In addition, laughing off discrimination in an often-lighthearted manner undermines the seriousness nature of the discrimination itself. Delegitimizing the negative component of discrimination through humor may therefore inadvertently be a poor strategy for benefiting the trans community as a whole. For individuals, humor was most often a short-term strategy to ensure temporary survival until they could make a substantial change in the workplace situation, usually via quitting.

It's the Job That Counts

Many participants also explained that in order to avoid discrimination, they intentionally chose jobs, working environments, and positions that would minimize negative treatment. Many looked specifically for explicitly LGBT-friendly workplaces, workplaces low in face-to-face interaction, or self-employment as strategies for reducing or avoiding discrimination. When workplace policies supported gender-diverse people in expressing themselves authentically in the workplace, participants often experienced short-term and long-term benefits. Additionally, because they were able to visibly demonstrate a variety of authentic gender-diverse identities and expressions, workplaces with trans-inclusive workplace policies positively affect the trans community. For the vast majority of the other strategies, which often involved choosing jobs in which trans individuals would be less noticed or interact with others less often, reductions of discrimination were also significant. However, because these strategies worked by reducing the visibility of gender-diverse people in the workplace, it tended to have a negligible to negative effect on the larger trans community by specifically keeping nonbinary and genderfluid people invisible and by concealing instances of discrimination.

Trans-Inclusive Policies

Several participants intentionally gained employment at workplaces that had trans-friendly policies in the hopes that these workplaces would be less discriminatory. Some of these workplaces had clearly delineated transition policies, while others had vocal LGBT internal groups or explicitly served LGBT populations.

Finding companies with trans-friendly policies was often a difficult task, but for those interviewees who successfully obtained employment at these companies, all experienced positive short- and long-term benefits. Individual benefits include being able to express themselves authentically, increased levels of confidence and happiness, and increased feelings of safety and comfort at work. In addition, workplaces with trans-inclusive policies benefit the larger trans community by supporting trans rights through an institutionalized acceptance of gender-nonconformity.

Low Face-to-Face Interaction

When interviewees couldn't find workplaces with trans-inclusive policies, many chose instead to work in environments with little face-to-face contact with coworkers and clients, citing this strategy as a good way to avoid discrimination. Like other strategies in which gender-diverse people sought to circumvent discrimination by modifying interactions in the workplace, choosing jobs with little contact with other workers reduced their visibility in the labor market. While limiting the potential to benefit the trans community through visibility, this strategy provides individual benefit by allowing interviewees to authentically express their gender without fear of gender policing or discrimination.

These interviewees all indicated that choosing jobs with low face-to-face interactions was generally desirable due to a lack of harassment and discrimination in response to their gender identity or expression. Choosing jobs with limited interpersonal interactions, whether with coworkers or clients, was a strategy that was often effective in the short term and long term for reducing workplace discrimination.

Self-Employment

In a similar vein, several interviewees chose self-employment as a strategy to avoid discrimination. Self-employment for many, while difficult to sustain in the long term, offered safety and comfort that other jobs and workplaces may not have had. That being said, these jobs were often less lucrative than traditional jobs, and so the cost of this strategy was often financial. Interviewees in this book often viewed it as a temporary strategy that was most effective in the short term. Like other strategies that decreased the visibility of gender-diverse people in the workplace, self-employment neither hurt nor benefited the larger trans community.

Avoid Filing Complaints

Many employees find themselves afraid to file an official complaint for fear that it will have repercussions for their careers in the future. Gender-diverse people often feel particularly afraid of the consequences of filing a complaint regarding trans discrimination, worrying that others will view them as being overly reactive, unyielding, or radical in their requests regarding how they want their gender to be treated in the workplace. Choosing to not file a complaint was an unsuccessful strategy in the short term but was employed in hopes of long-term benefit by avoiding incurring a negative reputation. This strategy is generally harmful for the larger trans community because it leaves discrimination experiences undocumented and unaddressed. Not only does this reduce the visibility of trans discrimination in the labor market, it also prevents the type of education that would lead an awareness of trans rights that could reduce discrimination for future gender-diverse employees. Concealing negative experiences may have generally contributed to perceptions that gender-diverse people do not consider instances of discrimination against them to be discrimination. Choosing not to file complaints may have also indicated to discriminatory individuals that their actions were excusable, which may negatively affect their future interactions with gender-diverse people.

Support Systems

Many of the participants in this book utilized resources and support systems in their communities and workplaces to combat or reduce discrimination. Often these support systems, including LGBT organizations, human resources, and in-work network connections, were effective in creating short-term and long-term benefits for the individual. Support systems that assist gender-diverse people in handling discrimination also benefit the wider trans community by promoting awareness of trans issues and demonstrating trans allyship.

LGBT Organizations

LGBT organizations often provide much-needed resources to gender-diverse people and often connect individuals to local programs offering support. The Trans Employment Project, which aims to provide employment support for gender-diverse people, was a particularly useful resource for many of the people interviewed. Other organizations provided vocational training, helped interviewees prepare for job fairs, connected interviewees to professionals, and provided social and community services.

These interviewees described their appreciation of these support systems, and often expressed hope that utilizing the resources available there would lead to professional benefit. Making use of these support systems was often a successful strategy in the short term and long term for the individual, and positively affected the larger trans community through promoting the success and well-being of its members and justifying the need for these important organizations.

Legal Name and Gender Change

Several participants sought the support of the legal system in approving their legal name and gender changes in an effort to legitimize their gender identities and provide a legal barrier to discrimination. While providing individual benefit in discrimination reduction, the strategy of prioritizing a legal name and gender change has a potentially negative effect on the trans community by normalizing legalization as a mandatory requirement in avoiding discrimination. Regardless, this strategy often greatly helped interviewees avoid discrimination in the short and long term.

Without a legal name and gender change, trans people often face uncomfortable workplace situations. Having documentation that affirms an individual's gender identity, however, can act like a shield that protects gender-diverse people from outright discrimination. One of the most vivid experiences in this vein concerns Robin, a white trans woman in her fifties, who described a harrowing experience in which her legal paperwork protected her from a potential discrimination experience regarding a security guard policing her bathroom usage. "[Discrimination] was such a big fear of mine that . . . I carried that ID on me for about the first six months I had it . . . I came walking out of the bathroom, and [a security guard] was standing in the doorway, and he weighed about 250 pounds, about 6.5 feet tall, he said, 'You know you are in the ladies room,' and I went, 'Of course I do, I'm a woman.' And he goes, 'Yeah, right,' and I pulled my license out, and he, went 'Oh shit, it's real,' like I was going to show him a fake ID. When I pulled it out, he literally thought I was going to show him a fake ID." After Robin displayed her ID, the security guard "turned white, because he realized that he just discriminated and harassed a woman, and that pretty much could get him fired, and he immediately apologized and profusely so."

Having a legal name and gender that matches an individual's perceived gender identity at work often protected gender-diverse people from workplace discrimination and negative treatment in both the short term and long term. However, the necessity of these legal changes may negatively affect the larger trans community by disadvantaging those who do not desire or do not have the ability to legally change their name and gender.

Human Resources

Making use of the HR in their individual workplaces was another common strategy many interviewees used to reduce discrimination and negative workplace experiences. However, results from utilizing HR varied widely across the participants in this book. While some participants reported experiences with their company's HR offering beneficial support, others reported HR itself as a site of discrimination.

Some participants who began transitioning while maintaining employment report HR being a helpful resource that legitimized their transition by providing resources to others and following a clearly set transition procedure. Other interviewees had positive experiences with their HR departments, but were unsuccessful at utilizing HR to reduce discrimination in the workplace due to unsupportive workplace environments or transphobic supervisors. Other interviewees mentioned HR departments that seemed to care very little about improving their workplace experiences. One interviewee, finally, reported experiencing discrimination directly from an HR representative.

Though utilizing HR departments was a strategy many participants utilized, whether or not the strategy was successful was often contingent on whether or not the overall workplace environment or company was trans-friendly to begin with. In environments with supportive policies, HR was often successful in further reducing discrimination by legitimizing and supporting trans identities in the workplace and by educating others through providing trans-awareness and sensitivity training to employees. In unsupportive workplaces, however, even if interviewees reported positive relationships with their HR departments, they were often unsuccessful at experiencing reductions in workplace discrimination. Overall, the strategy of relying on HR departments to reduce discrimination was a positive strategy for the greater trans community by promoting visibility of trans people in the workplace and trans-awareness education.

Friends and Connections

Interviewees often relied on their personal connections to secure employment and as protection from discrimination within the workplace. Several interviewees found job offers with the support of their network, as friends', family's, and past employers' recommendations seemed to counteract the trans status discrimination in hiring that these interviewees may have faced. This strategy of utilizing networks to secure employment is beneficial to the individual in the short and long term as well as to the larger trans community by supporting the visibility of gender-diverse people, especially those who otherwise experienced intense difficulty obtaining employment.

Many indicated that having cisgender friends inside a workplace offered them some protection from discrimination on the job, as well. Friends played a large role in setting the standard for coworkers' interactions by visibly reinforcing gender-diverse people's identities, and modeling how coworkers ought to respond to gender-diverse employees. This allows gender-diverse people more access to more workplace opportunities and grants them greater respect. Additionally, these friends can ensure that experiences of discrimination are swiftly addressed.

Whether in order to obtain employment or to reduce discrimination, networking was often a highly successful strategy for the individual in both the short and the long term. The presence of helpful allies in a workplace who legitimized gender-diverse people identities and expressions protects them from discrimination and allows them to be visible and authentic within their respective workplaces. Networking has a strong positive effect on the trans community by increasing visibility and providing a strong model of trans allyship.

CONCLUSION

Gender-diverse people utilize a wide variety of tactics and strategies to reduce discrimination in the workplace. Some of these strategies are intended to reduce short-term negative treatment, while others aim for more long-term improvement; some of these strategies focus on improving circumstances for the individuals while other focus on improving conditions for the trans community as a whole.[1] While strategies that provide short-term benefits often focus on temporary, subtle modifications to some aspect one's gender expression that is causing conflict in the workplace, our analysis of participant interviews reveals that these strategies often require individual compromises that are unsustainable in the long term. Because many strategies that focus on short-term benefits may also seek to limit confrontation, instances of discrimination often continue. Long-term benefits tend to result from strategies that allow authentic expressions of gender identity and presentation, like coming out in the workplace (Ceperich and Hash 2006; Day and Schoenrade 1997). Strategies intended to produce long-term benefits often require a higher level of cooperation in the workplace between the employee and the employer than strategies producing short-term benefits. Few strategies with the potential for long-term benefits exist because of workplaces with high levels of discrimination and situations where employer–employee cooperation is either too risky to attempt or unlikely to succeed.

This research also reveals that while individuals may use successful strategies to reduce discrimination against the self, these strategies often maintain or increase discrimination against the trans community as a whole. Gender-diverse people are often caught in a vicious cycle where their survival and well-being in the workplace is contingent on conforming to inauthentic perceptions of trans identity and expression, while their conformity itself reinforces these unrealistic perceptions. With regard to discrimination-reducing strategies, many gender-diverse people are often caught in a prisoner's dilemma— what is most beneficial for a gender-diverse individual may not be best for the overall trans community with regard to trans inclusivity and rights in the labor market, and vice versa. For the sake of their own safety and success, many gender-diverse people are motivated

---

[1]There are many different trans communities that may organize around shared race, socioeconomic status, industry, or experiences. Each community has different needs, and it is presumptuous to combine and reduce them all into the idea of one monolithic trans community. As a reminder, however, we sometimes use the term as shorthand to describe the general populations of trans people in their many communities.

to take actions that may have unintended negative consequences for the wider community (Lorah and Pepper 2008). We acknowledge that individuals vary widely in motivations and intent regarding the strategies they employ. While some of these research participants explicitly indicated their conflict between supporting the self and supporting the community, others did not indicate that supporting the larger trans community was a priority and therefore employed primarily self-beneficial strategies.

Gender-diverse people who employed discrimination-reduction strategies grappled with often-conflicting motivations between individual short-term benefits and long-term benefits and between individual and community benefits. In general, strategies that decreased interviewees' visibility in the workplace and involved modifying gender expression to adhere with workplace cultures have the potential to offer discrimination reduction for the individual but not the wider trans community. Strategies that increased interviewees' visibility in the workplace and allowed them to express their identity in authentic ways tended to benefit the individual as well as the trans community. The more trans-friendly a workplace, as measured by trans-inclusive policies and available resources for gender-diverse people, the more potential visibility-increasing strategies have to produce long-term individual and community benefits.

Participants in this research utilized a wide range of strategies in an effort to avoid or reduce discrimination in the workplace. These strategies ranged from concealing their gender identities and modifying their gender expressions to modifying interactions in the workplace, to intentionally choosing jobs that would be less discriminatory, and to utilizing workplace-specific or external support systems to reduce negative treatment. The experiences of interviewees strongly suggest that the quality of the workplace environment is a major predictor of not only discrimination experiences, but also the degree of success different strategies are able to achieve in reducing discrimination.

In workplaces without trans-inclusive policies, workplaces in which managers and administrators were prejudiced, or workplaces with unfriendly working environments, gender-diverse participants were more likely to conceal their identity or modify their expressions in order to pass as gender-normative. These strategies were often focused on avoiding attention and conforming to more gender-normative identities and expressions. These strategies were often successful for many participants in the short term, especially with regard to the hiring process. For nonbinary and genderfluid people, modifying gender expression toward binary stereotypes in order to pass as gender-normative is an unsuccessful strategy in the long term because a nonbinary or fluid presentation is essential for an authentic gender expression. Additionally, when participants chose to hide their trans identities or express their gender in an inauthentic manner, strategies of concealing identities and modifying expressions in the workplace had no beneficial effect on the larger trans community due to the inability for invisible trans identities to positively change workplace or societal perceptions of gender-nonconformity.

Individuals who were not able to pass as gender-normative or who were otherwise unwilling to hide their nonconforming gender identities or expressions often modified their interpersonal interactions as a strategy for reducing workplace discrimination. These antidiscrimination strategies tended to offer short-term benefits but were often unsustainable in the long run if it required an individual to compromise their desire for authenticity within their workplace. Many participants chose to present their trans identities within narrow ranges deemed acceptable by unfriendly workplaces, sought to reduce conflict as much as possible, and attempted to avoid interaction with others in the workplace by choosing jobs with minimal contact among coworkers and clients. These strategies were often successful in helping participants in this study be visibly gender-diverse while still maintaining employment. However, they often required people to reinforce stereotypical and harmful notions of trans identity in the workplace. As a result, these strategies often contribute to an overall negative impact on the larger trans community because they allow these harmful notions of trans identity to become the standards by which trans people are evaluated in almost any environment in which a trans identity is salient. By perpetuating inaccurate ideas of what it means to be a trans person in the workplace, individual trans people inadvertently motivate others in the community to perpetuate the same stereotypes in order to avoid discrimination.

Many interviewees intentionally sought to gain employment at workplaces that would lend themselves to less discrimination. For some, these workplaces had trans-inclusive policies, while for others, these workplaces primarily involved solitary work. This strategy led to short-term and, if sustainable, long-term benefits in workplace treatment. These strategies tended to have a negligible impact on the greater trans community because while they provided employment for trans individuals, they also often led to a lack of visibility of gender-diverse workers in the labor market.

Workplace-based support systems were more effective in reducing discrimination in trans-friendly workplace environments with explicit trans-inclusive policies and supportive coworkers and management. In addition, trans-friendly workplace environments were more likely to support authentic and visible expressions of gender identity than less friendly workplace environments. Colleagues in the latter environment pressured interviewees to suppress authentic gender expression and conceal gender-nonconformity. In unfriendly workplaces, utilizing workplace support systems like HR and even external support systems like local trans-friendly programs was a strategy that achieved only limited, often short-term, success. Most participants were unable to find workplaces that were ideal in terms of trans-friendly policies, management, and working environment; as a result, many struggled to navigate less-than-ideal workplaces and heavily compromised their own gender identities or expressions in order to survive. The threat of unemployment led many to value obtaining and retaining a job more than anything else, and several participants who had initially been authentic in their workplace presentation eventually chose to hide their identities and modify gender expressions in favor of employment.

AFAB people, whether butch women, trans men, or AFAB nonbinary people, described discrimination-reduction strategies far less often than trans women and AMAB nonbinary/genderfluid people. This discrepancy is strongly linked to our findings showing that more masculine participants received less discrimination, experienced less pressure to present differently, and felt less motivation to compromise their identities and expressions, while nonmasculine AFAB interviewees were able to pass as cisgender women and avoid discrimination that way. Because hegemonic masculine gender expressions and interactional styles are favored in workplaces, individuals who perform these forms of masculinity have far less need to utilize discrimination-reducing strategies.

Also consistent with our findings, assigned male at birth nonbinary and genderfluid participants, who experienced the most discrimination in the workplace, engaged in the most strategies to reduce discrimination. Though some workplaces were supportive of binary notions of transitioning and trans identity, very few were friendly toward nonbinary or genderfluid participants, who were often forced to hide their gender identities or modify their expressions in order to gain and retain employment. As a result, those trans people who are generally the most visible in the workplace tend to be trans men and trans women, who often aim to pass as cisgender with varying degrees of success. The effect that this lopsided representation has among the industries in which trans people work and on the larger trans community is the reinforcement of the idea that nonbinary and genderfluid people do not exist in the labor market. This lack of representation of nonbinary and genderfluid people fuels a vicious cycle of discrimination where nonbinary and genderfluid people are repeatedly treated like anomalies compared to the "normal" perception of trans identity limited to a spectrum of nonpassing and passing trans men and trans women. This discrimination has the end result of reproducing, reifying, and maintaining the existing paradigm.

Successful strategies for avoiding and reducing discrimination reveal not only the complexities of the existing status quo of discrimination, but also the ways in which discriminatory situations are self-perpetuating. The most successful strategies for reducing discrimination serve to reinforce both the gender binary and the dominance of hegemonic masculinity in the workplace. Though each individual acts primarily to better their own situation in the workplace, the macro-level effect of these individual actions is the reinforcing of binary notions of gender that reward only certain strategies for only certain individuals. Trans women experience the most success in reducing discrimination when they adhere to the "born in the wrong body" narrative and reinforce notions that a transition must be binary as well as socially, physiologically, and legally confirmed in order to be legitimate. Nonbinary and genderfluid people experience the most success in reducing discrimination when they "pick one" gender identity by adhering consistently to notions that gender identity and expression should be both binary and fixed. While doing ambiguity is a means of legitimizing nonbinary identities, many individuals are discouraged from doing ambiguity as it often results in discrimination. In all of these situations, individuals often must conform to systemic ideas that negatively affect the trans community in order to protect themselves within the workplace. While some of these strategies are successful in the short and long term for certain individuals—mainly trans people who feel authentic in their performance of a binary gender expression—for many, choosing visibility and authenticity in the workplace is tantamount to unemployment, harassment, and discrimination.

It may be that the trade-offs established here—maximum visibility is maximally helpful for the trans community while maximally taxing for trans individuals, and minimum visibility is minimally helpful for the trans community while minimally taxing for trans individuals—do not fully account for all successful discrimination-reducing strategies. Instead, it may be that the trans people who are most able to make an impact are the ones who are gender-diverse in a moderate manner. Meyerson and Tompkins (2007) describe these "tempered radicals" as "individuals who identify with and are committed to their organizations, and are also committed to a cause, community, or ideology that is fundamentally different from, and possibly at odds with, the dominant culture of their organization[s]" (311). These actors have particular power to influence change within organizations if they are able to remain "anchored in distinct communities or institutions to resist the cooptation pressures marginalized individuals face as they gain legitimacy in a dominant institution" (319). Therefore, trans people who are only moderately gender-diverse may be able to access sufficient legitimacy to create change in the workplace without receiving backlash as a result of having a highly non-normative gender identity or expression. The framework that Meyerson and Tompkins provide gives insight into the complex nature of the diverse discrimination-reduction strategies available.

In this research, only a handful of discrimination-reducing strategies were successful for both the individual and the community. Crucially, these strategies relied on preexisting situational factors that made workplace discrimination reduction possible in the short and long term, allowed gender-diverse individuals to be authentic in the workplace, and positively affected the larger trans community through challenging misconceptions and celebrating visibility. Apart from the presence of trans-inclusive workplace policies, which tended to primarily benefit binary-identifying trans people, the largest situational factor that predicted this type of far-reaching discrimination reduction was the presence of authority figures that legitimized and supported authentic gender-diverse identities and expressions in the workplace. The few interviewees who were supported in this way described workplace experiences that were significantly less discriminatory than the many who were not, and enjoyed a greater level of authenticity in the workplace than most.

CHAPTER SEVEN

Moving Forward

Our interviewees described a range of discrimination experiences across a large number of organizations caused by ignorance, negligence, fear, and/or prejudice. We have traced each instance of discrimination to those mechanisms that we believe caused them and from there sought to understand how and why such discrimination happens.

Let's return to the question of "Why trans-inclusivity?" Trans people are both a minority and a marginalized population, with unique needs to be met before they can survive, let alone thrive, in a workplace environment. In light of the extreme difficulties of supporting trans employees, what does an organization have to gain by embracing trans inclusivity, especially if doing so is neither popular nor convenient?

To answer this question, we draw on the idea of corporate social responsibility (CSR), a business model whereby organizations distribute resources into activities related to environmental or social well-being. CSR perspectives argue that by investing in employees, communities, and consumers, organizations can create long-term profit and better community relations and contribute to societal well-being in general.

A CSR perspective in relation to trans inclusivity might first recommend inclusivity from the perspective of risk management. As trans people and trans communities gain greater visibility, an organization stands to suffer negative hits to its reputation, public perception, and profits as a result of any high-profile cases of discrimination, lawsuits, or otherwise negative press. By proactively adopting trans-inclusive policies—especially where nondiscrimination law exists and local communities are highly aware of trans issues—an organization can save itself large sums of money and reputation with a relatively small investment.

The value of the CSR perspective, however, lies mostly in the perspective of inclusivity for the sake of value creation. By seeing trans-inclusivity as not simply an obligation to cover an organization's liabilities but as a positive characteristic that adds value by its own right, organizations can stand to benefit from becoming more inclusive.

The canon of diversity literature and research holds, generally, that a more diverse workplace population increases access to information, innovation, and creativity at the cost of group cohesiveness. In other words, the more diverse the group, the less alike its members will think and the less its members will get along with each other. From the perspective of trans-inclusivity, which aims to integrate and support trans people, this suggests that merely inserting trans people into workplaces is unlikely to do much good for any organization; indeed, many trans employees we interviewed seemed so uncomfortable in their workplace environments that it was difficult to imagine their presence adding much to their organizations. This suggests to us that organizations cannot take shortcuts to trans-inclusivity—for an organization to truly benefit from the insights of trans employees, it must first do the work to create workplace policies and workplace cultures that allow trans employees to feel safe and supported. When trans employees feel a sense of psychological safety in the workplace, they are far more able to feel safe, speaking their mind, putting forth novel ideas, and challenging old ways of thinking.

In a trans-inclusive organization that instills in trans employees this sense of psychological safety, we can imagine trans employees being able to contribute truly unique insights in an organizational setting— for example, nonbinary or genderfluid employees may be able to offer insights beyond the binary on aspects of organizations that would otherwise be taken for granted, like advertising, client relationships, workplace dynamics, and policies. Including trans employees allows for the unique life experiences they have experienced to contribute to workplace innovation, creativity, and success, making inclusivity appealing for its own sake. Organizations that embrace it are likely to enjoy not only a competitive advantage in their industries, but also positive regard and patronage from trans communities and LGBTQ+ organizations.

We believe that the case for trans-inclusivity is compelling and relevant for many organizations today. Yet clearly, from those experiences we have documented in this book, much work remains until organizations are truly welcoming and inclusive for trans people. What can we do to make things better? What are some concrete solutions we can adopt toward trans-inclusivity?

Finding even small steps to take can feel at times like an impossible task. We have documented trans discrimination exhaustively, revealing the many ways in which it can be subtle or blatant, manipulative or violent, individual or systemic. No one-size-fits-all approach to change could ever address the many varied ways in which discrimination plays out in the workplace, but we have nevertheless sought to compile a set of policy recommendations that we believe encompasses and addresses a large variety of trans discrimination.

These recommendations must be the start—not the end—of a conversation that goes far beyond our book. Not every recommendation will be applicable in every situation; not every instance of trans discrimination in a workplace will fit into the categories we've laid out. We cannot forget that policy change is just one component of something bigger, just a small part of societal change, cultural change, and institutional change, all of which are essential to trans communities' well-being. This is something we must all keep in mind—whether we embrace these recommendations for the sake of ideology, profit, community, or necessity. Policy change cannot and should not be the end of advocacy efforts—it is simply one essential component of what justice for trans people looks like.

THE UNWILLING ORGANIZATION

Many of the organizations trans people seek or find employment in have no desire to make their workplaces trans-inclusive. While the most egregious of these organizations may have explicit transphobia institutionalized through policy and practices, most display their disdain for trans people by simply doing nothing at all. Many trans people who seek to enter these workplaces never make it past the interview process, especially if their gender expressions deviate from the norm. Those who do enter these organizations must struggle to survive. Supervisors and authority figures at these organizations may turn a blind eye to harassment or violence on the job, or even participate in it themselves. Human resources or other sources of accountability in the workplace may scorn or ignore trans employees who experience discrimination, future isolating them. When we describe organizations as "unwilling to move toward trans-inclusivity," we do so with the understanding that there is no singular organization we seek to characterize. Some organizations span many workplaces while others are small family-owned businesses; some are led by a transphobic leaders who actively oppose inclusivity while others are led by those who are simply ignorant about trans people even existing at all. These organizations differ widely in size, industry, and structure, yet share in common a distinct lack of concern toward trans people and trans employees.

Nondiscrimination Law

While our book focuses on the San Francisco Bay Area, we nevertheless collected a number of stories of trans people working in other geopolitical locations without nondiscrimination law protecting gender identity. Kai, a white transmasculine person in his thirties, was forced out of his veterinarian clinic in Arizona when he began to transition on the job. When he went to the HR department, he was told that he "could kiss his ass goodbye because he had no rights in Arizona." Where legislation protecting trans people is lacking, organizations often have little motivation to offer even minimal support to their trans employees. Trans people living in these areas may face pervasive unemployment, and trans people within organizations may delay coming out or transitioning indefinitely so as to keep their jobs. Trans people who choose to report discrimination may find their claims dismissed or their investigations neglected, and can face heavy and swift retaliation from their employers that often leads to termination.

While the Equal Employment Opportunity Commission has ruled multiple times that Title VII prohibits discrimination on the bases of both sexual orientation and gender identity, these rulings apply only to public employees. While many cities in a variety of states have laws that extend this protection to local employees, many more do not. In 30 states, no employment nondiscrimination laws exist that protect employees on the basis of gender identity, with 3 of these states additionally preventing enforcement of federal nondiscrimination laws. Organizations and advocacy groups across the nation that fight for nondiscrimination laws protecting trans people often encounter stiff resistance. Much of the conservative pushback against such legislation stems from unfounded fears and misconceptions of trans people as sexually deviant, predatory, morally lacking, or unnatural; trans people are seen as undesirables that do not belong in workplaces, and do not deserve protection.

While protective laws are by no means panaceas for trans discrimination, they act as important legal structure and firm ground for trans employees and advocacy groups to continue lobbying and working toward trans inclusivity in workplaces and beyond. *We recommend that those campaigns, advocacy groups, and lobbyists working toward trans-inclusivity continue to push for nondiscrimination legislation in all states.*

Providing this legal framework for nondiscrimination allows advocacy groups to get their feet in the doors of otherwise unwilling organizations, and is a strong launching-off point for any trans-inclusivity campaign.

Reporting Processes

Included in the realm of nondiscrimination law must be state- and federal-level reporting processes that help resolve and investigate claims of trans discrimination in a fair and timely manner. In organizations not committed to supporting trans employees, internal procedures for reporting and resolving trans discrimination are almost always lacking. Trans employees who face discrimination must either seek help from external sources or not seek help at all. If the state or locality trans employees work in does not have nondiscrimination laws established, then reporting discrimination is unlikely to result in any resolution. Yet, even the presence of nondiscrimination law does not guarantee a fair or timely investigation or resolution of discrimination claims.

Because reporting processes and procedures for discrimination complaints vary state by state and sometimes city by city, it is unlikely that generalized recommendations for structural changes will be easily applied across different localities. What most of these reporting processes share in common, however, is the presence of an individual or individuals who determine whether a submitted claim is accepted for investigation. *We recommend, therefore, that all investigators, interviewers, and those responsible for approving these claims—whether federal, state, or third-party agents—undergo comprehensive training on trans workplace discrimination.* These trainings would ideally be based upon a standardized set of materials compiled by a national-level trans advocacy group or groups, with additions as necessary made by local- or state-level trans advocacy groups, and would cover types and experiences of discrimination unique to trans people that those responsible for approving discrimination claims would need to know.

Third-Party Pressure

Benchmarks like the Human Rights Campaign's Corporate Equality Index (CEI) are a useful tool for prompting many organizations to adopt more LGBTQ+ friendly policies. However, in areas where the majority of organizations and employers do not care about LGBTQ

communities or employees, such indexes are extremely limited in use-
fulness. Trans people looking for employment may not have the ability
to choose employers with a higher CEI rating, if such ratings are even
available—for those who must pick between equally prejudiced or
unsafe organizations to work for, these indexes do not help.

While many organizations may scorn or otherwise dismiss trans
advocacy groups, many of these same organizations place a premium
on industry-specific metrics or standards. Whether construction firms,
health clinics, or manufacturing shops, many professions carry out
business with industry standards of safety, routine, and policy in
mind. Putting explicit protections for trans employees within those
industry standards pressures all employers in those industries to at
least think critically about making their workplaces more trans-
inclusive, whether or not federal or state legislation exists. In a similar
vein, third-party watchdogs often apply additional pressure to industries to make their workplaces more desirable to work in. Including
treatment of trans employees among the evaluation criteria is a subtle
but important step in changing workplace environments, and at the
very least increases the visibility of trans employees and their issues
to employers that would otherwise not be aware of them.

The decentralized nature of this work suggests that it be best tackled
by trans people and advocates for trans inclusivity already situated
within different industries. *We recommend that lobbyists and activists
campaign for third-party organizations and industry leaders to adopt protections for trans employees within their evaluation criteria and industry standards.* Industry leaders who attract a large following or command
substantial influence within their fields are able to galvanize change,
especially in industries or organizations that care more about intra-
industry competition than federal or state regulations. Influencing
these leaders to adopt trans-inclusivity policies has the potential for
major ripple effects in industry standards and wide-scale social
change.

Education

Common across many organizations, unwilling to move toward
trans inclusivity is a widespread lack of accurate information on trans
identity, trans communities, and trans issues. Many employers may
simply not be familiar with trans employees, and may reject them
out of discomfort, unfamiliarity, or desire to avoid complications.
Other employers may hold active prejudices against trans people,
believing falsely that trans people are inherently criminal, sexually

perverted, unprofessional, undesirable incompetent, or otherwise unfit for employment. Kelly, a white trans woman in her sixties who despite her experience had been largely unemployed since coming out as a trans woman, makes this point when she said, "If [employers] got a choice, why take the queer when you got a perfectly good something else?" Many of these negative perceptions of trans people are subtly taught through constant negative representations of trans people in mass media and not-so-subtly taught by politicians, talk-show hosts, and other influential individuals who propagate and take advantage of these misconceptions to restrict trans youth from school facilities, deny trans people health procedures, and otherwise limit and marginalize trans communities. We strongly believe that no organization unwilling to support trans employees will become willing through the use of external pressure alone, but that external pressure can make the work of education more accessible and effective.

Education is necessary because the question of "why should I support trans people?" requires more than legal obligation and the threat of punishment as answers. Forcing an organization uncommitted to inclusivity to adopt inclusive policy is an ineffective solution: with little oversight, these organizations will dodge and skimp on policy; with heavy oversight, these organizations will be unmotivated and inefficient. While educating employers and organizations is by no means a speedy solution to what is a larger sociocultural problem, it is an unavoidable step in changing organizations' outlook on trans employees.

The topic of education is an extensive one, and one we will revisit later this chapter. As it relates to organizations unwilling to become more trans-inclusive, education is necessary to replace people's negative, stereotypical, and inaccurate representations of trans people— as sexually deviant, predatory, morally lacking, undesirable, and unprofessional—with more realistic ones. The difficulty of such a recommendation, however, lies in creating a program, training, or intervention that can effectively change beliefs and attitudes using a realistic allocation of resources.

In a review of existing prejudice reduction literature, Paluck and Green (2009) found that the vast majority of interventions were unable to successfully reduce both implicit and explicit prejudice over a significant period of time. However, they cite Cook's Contact Hypothesis studies (1978, 1984) and interventions involving narrative persuasion (Zillman 1991) as being prime examples of effective interventions. In other words, spending time with individuals of marginalized groups and hearing real narratives and stories from and about individuals of those groups can change negative beliefs. Paluck and Green suggest that such belief change should take place in environments of "cooperative learning," where members of a group or organization are allowed to learn together, at their own pace. How can such an environment be created within an organization reluctant to change its culture or collective attitude toward trans people?

We propose that states and/or localities require trans-specific content within compliance trainings, effectively making this kind of education mandatory. Local trans advocacy groups can work to streamline content related to trans inclusivity such that it retains its effectiveness (through storytelling and outgroup contact) without becoming overly prescriptive. The goal of these trainings should not be to singlehandedly turn an unfriendly organization into a model organization for trans-inclusivity, but to instead move the topic of trans-inclusivity into a more politically neutral space, such that organizations might be willing to consider additional training or programming in the future.

In addition, we propose that trans advocacy groups specifically target industry leaders and influential figures to offer educational trainings and workshops. The goal of these educational trainings or workshops is significantly different from those suggested to be part of compliance training; education aimed at these individuals must have the goal of convincing them not only that trans people deserve fair treatment but also that trans people have unique strengths, skills, and knowledge that make them uniquely valuable and positive additions to workplaces. Advocates can argue also that since a more diverse workplace improves access to information, creative problem-solving skills, and solution generation, organizations, workplaces, and entire industries can stand to benefit by embracing and valuing the novel insights provided by trans employees. By gaining allies in industry leaders, advocates for trans inclusivity can apply pressure to organizations within those industries who look toward industry leaders for guidance.

INCLUSION IN PROGRESS

Organizations that state an intent or goal of becoming more trans-inclusive have taken a large step, but many difficulties and challenges still exist to turn their intentions into impact into inclusion. As the trans people we interviewed described with painstaking detail, often times even those organizations that professed strong support for trans people routinely treated their trans employees in unfair, dehumanizing, exhausting, and discriminating ways. Many tried to limit their trans employees' contact with clients or the public in general, causing employees to feel stigmatized and undervalued. Many placed restrictions on trans employees' gender expressions or even gender identities in the workplace, causing employees to feel unsupported, inauthentic, and stressed at work. Almost all of the trans people we interviewed reported some kind of subtle discrimination from their employers or coworkers, even if those individuals making disparaging remarks or insensitive statements were themselves unaware that they were doing so. Organizations that profess friendliness toward trans people may continue to be harmful or unsafe for their trans employees for a number of reasons. Some adhere to a workplace culture that unintentionally stigmatizes and marginalizes those employees who do not "fit in," for whatever reason. Some may lack the institutional knowledge to know how to properly treat trans employees, and leave trans people in those organizations at the mercy of their supervisors. Or perhaps the organization's workforce may simply not believe in the same things as its leaders, and hampers inclusivity efforts due to unconscious bias or prejudice. There are many ways in which organizations can improve with regard to truly becoming trans-inclusive, and we present a number of them based on our research.

Supervisors as Beacons of Support

The trans people we interviewed had a vast range of experiences in different workplaces and industries, but nearly all of them mentioned their supervisors or managers in some way. Many trans people reported negative experiences: supervisors learning about their trans identities through paperwork and harassing them as a result; supervisors controlling their bathroom usage, workplace attire, and access to resources; and supervisors turning a blind eye to workplace discrimination and refusing to support trans employees. But on the other side of these grim stories of prejudice and discrimination are positive narratives of supervisor support, when supervisors stick up for their trans employees and by doing so set an example for the entire workplace to do the same. Cassidy, an Asian American transmasculine person in their twenties, described a supervisor at a law firm who "would say to the other . . . associate attorneys like, 'Oh, this is Cassidy. He's doing this' and so people would follow his lead." Even though Cassidy's workplace lacked any explicit protections for trans employees, this show of support by his supervisor set a workplace norm of respecting Cassidy's pronouns and trans identity, which single-handedly made Cassidy's workplace experience positive.

Supervisors can easily be the single-most deciding factor of a trans employee's workplace experiences—perhaps even more so than trans-inclusive policies. An unsupportive supervisor, manager, or other authority figure often has the power to make a job miserable by sabotaging support, restricting promotion, and otherwise using influence to negatively impact trans employees. We were struck particularly by the experience of Kai, a white transmasculine person in his thirties, who enlisted the support of a friendly HR representative after being discriminated against. Rather than support and help him, Kai's boss had that representative replaced with a far less sympathetic person, and relentlessly drove Kai out of the job.

Investing in inclusion means investing in supportive supervisors, supervisors who understand the unique challenges trans people face in the workplace and are willing to take the lead in creating trans-friendly workplace environments. These supervisors often understand that trans people are not troubled employees who need to be protected, but rather employees whose unique skills and talents require first a sense of psychological safety in the workplace. By proactively creating these workplace environments, trans-inclusive managers allow trans employees to be their authentic selves and thrive in any organization—especially so because a trans-inclusive manager signals the expected conduct of a workplace and models norms of respect that other employees themselves take on. In other words, trans-inclusive managers are not shields but platforms that provide trans employees with safety and firm ground to excel and perform in many organizations.

We recommend that organizations committed to trans-inclusivity add trans-friendliness to evaluation criteria used for both supervisors' hiring and promotion processes. Such criteria should evaluate their attitudes toward leadership, leadership approaches toward people of all identities in the workplace, and commitments to fostering a productive, supportive, and positive workplace environment for all people. By doing so, organizations can signal that trans-inclusivity is valued and that supervisors are expected to play a significant part in creating a workplace culture that can support trans employees.

We recommend as well that organizations make internal commitments to hire trans people in management and other leadership positions. Too often, trans people are either not hired at all or hired and kept at entry- or near-entry-level positions. Alex, a highly qualified white trans woman in her forties, was told by a senior recruiter for a tech company, " 'Don't bother going through any recruiters because they're not going to touch you ... because you're trans.' ... Their job is to present, especially at the senior level, these perfect candidates. If they present a candidate that has any deficiencies it reflects on them as a recruiter."

As a result, trans employees rarely find themselves in positions where their unique skills and knowledge can have a significantly positive impact on shaping organizational goals, culture, and outcomes. Trans supervisors additionally have enormous influence as positive representation for trans people both inside and outside the organization, potentially encouraging other trans people to seek employment at the organization. This is a compelling solution to what many organizations complain about as a supply-side problem of lacking trans representation among the hiring pool: by hiring trans people into leadership positions, organizations can send a strong message that they respect and care about trans people as employees. We saw no better example than that of Robin, a white trans woman in her fifties who worked in a theater company. When she was intentionally called an "it" by a transphobic client, her trans supervisor immediately called out the client for his inappropriate behavior and refused to ever work with him again. "That makes me feel really good, when they support you like that," Robin explained. The support that Robin had from her trans supervisor left such an enormously positive reaction on her, and motivated her to keep working in that industry.

Better Resources for Human Resources

Despite the large influence that managers and supervisors have on the workplace experiences of trans employees, HR staff and specialists are responsible for a large degree of employee life in the form of discipline and conflict resolution, training, screening, and recruitment. If managers determine whether trans employees survive or thrive in the workplace, then HR sets the basic structural and institutional framework that enables this thriving to happen at all. For most organizations, HR will be the ones to consider, evaluate, and ultimately implement the recommendations we suggest here, weighing proposed changes to organizational routine, practice, or culture in terms of their impact to organizational performance and the organization's fulfillment of its unique goals. Due to the high importance of HR to trans-inclusive workplaces, we cannot overlook the causal influence of HR departments and teams themselves in enabling organizations to embrace inclusion.

Organizations looking to become more trans-inclusive must at some point in their efforts work through HR to implement new policies and procedures. *We recommend that HR work with organizational leaders push-ing change—if not drive change efforts themselves—to set effective and ambi-tious timelines for implementation of new policy.* By translating vague ideology (we should have more trans-friendly facilities) into concrete action plans (all buildings on this campus must have a gender-neutral bathroom in every wing of every floor, by February 10th), HR can set the tone and pace of implemented change. This is an easy rec-ommendation and takes little effort from HR for a large potential impact.

Many trans employees have unique workplace needs that necessi-tate HR to assist them. On logistical issues regarding payment, docu-mentation, and other procedural aspects of workplaces, trans people often face additional difficulties in the workplace when HR is unfamil-iar with trans-related policy, or if such policy does not exist in the first place. Blake, a mixed trans man in his twenties, explains, "I had to have my paperwork done two or three times . . . because [the HR representatives] weren't sure which documents I have to put legal name on and which documents they could put my given name on. They weren't sure what to put on my pay stubs. They weren't sure what to do with any of it. And so that was a pain." In many cases, this lack of familiarity with trans employees leads to significant workplace distress and additional experiences of discrimination, especially if HR is called upon to assist with workplace conflicts involving trans employees. Jessie, a Latinx nonbinary person in their forties, requested to be referred to by feminine pronouns but went to HR when their coworkers ignored this request. HR was useless in resolving the con-flict. When Jessie finally took the initiative and tried to take on the work of correcting and educating coworkers, Jessie was pushed to leave the workplace.

We recommend that national-level trans advocacy groups and organiza-tions create a universal document of recommended procedures and guidelines for helping trans employees, and share this document widely with existing HR departments in workplaces, human resource certification programs, and designers of human resource-related curriculum and resources. Such a docu-ment should include information including but not limited to: stan-dard procedures for employees who change their name, gender pronouns, and/or gender expression on the job; basic trainings on gender and sexuality education for any organization; and standard interview and recruitment etiquette and federal- and state-specific laws on reporting and documentation. This document could be a concise set of "trans-friendly best practices" that trans advocacy organizations distribute to business owners and other employers as first steps to including trans employees. For small businesses and other organizations where HR isn't present, this kind of resource could conveniently put relevant information for trans employees into one place and vastly increase the ability of such organizations to meet the logistical and workplace needs of trans people.

Gendered Spaces

In the last few years, many workplaces have begun offering unique spaces and event programming for different identity groups, most notably women, in the form of women's-only parties, women's self-defense courses, and women's workshops on succeeding in the workplace. All have contributed to bolstering women's communities in the workplace, especially in organizations where the gender ratio skews toward men. Women often have their own employee resource groups (ERGs), special event programming, and allocated funding for community-building in the workplace. By explicitly creating women's spaces, organizations acknowledge that having a stronger sense of community is essential in countering stereotype threat and helping women stand on more equal footing with men in the workplace.

Yet, strong women's networks in a workplace often create strong men's networks to mirror them. Women's spaces are matched by men's spaces, and gender binarism can be slowly but surely institutionalized into organizational structure. It is this very formalization of gendered workplace structures, networks, and spaces that may inadvertently marginalize or exclude trans employees.

Parker, a white trans man in his twenties, felt isolated from his coworkers when he was perceived to be a butch woman at his sales analyst job. "There was this kind of men's space here and women's space here; I just wasn't necessarily welcome more or less to either place," he explained. "I would kind of sit somewhere in the middle . . . and that was kind of othering in that way. So it was just kind of secret social space, I wasn't really allowed to bridge either."

While gendered network spaces can be beneficial for those ingroup members who use them, often times those who are excluded from these spaces, as Parker was, can feel highly marginalized and without community. For trans employees and employees who otherwise do not fit neatly into binary-gendered "men's" or "women's" spaces, these workplace structures may prevent workplace integration, exacerbate tensions, and cause trans employees to feel like they do not belong. *We recommend that organizations commit to creating an equal number of all-gendered spaces, events, and programming compared to those that are gendered.* By doing so, organizations can retain the beneficial nature of ERGs and other identity-specific communities without excluding those who do not fit neatly into them. Additionally, *we recommend that organizations nudge ERGs to explicitly include mention of trans people in their group descriptions, and actively strive to include trans employees.* That is, Asian American ERGs should make a larger effort to include Asian American trans people, disabled and neurodivergent ERGs should make a larger effort to include disabled and/or neurodivergent trans people, and so on. Making this proactive effort helps at least partially counter the tendency for trans people with multiple marginalized identities to be ostracized by even those with whom they share similar identities and experiences with.

Dress Codes

Another aspect of workplace life that unintentionally marginalize trans employees is workplace- or industry-mandated dress codes. While dress codes can be used to better foster a sense of workplace culture and community, gendered dress codes marginalize trans people and can even lead to their termination as a result of their gender-nonconformity or nonbinary gender identity. For Rowan, a white nonbinary person in their twenties, their gender expression was often critiqued by their HR representative: "was concerned about how I presented would impact other people's perception of the company. When we went to go do recruiting, she explicitly took me aside and told me things not to wear . . . 'Don't wear a dress, don't wear makeup' essentially present really consistently as far as you can." Rowan found that their managers in the workplace would question their competence and micromanage them more closely on days when their gender expression was more feminine—sending Rowan the firm message that looking a certain way in the workplace made them a target for discrimination. *We recommend that organizations strongly considered de-emphasizing workplace dress codes, and more strongly emphasizing those characteristics of workplace culture that are desired more directly.* For example, rather than using a conservative dress code to convey efficiency, formality, and dedication to clients, workplaces can more explicitly work to create cultures that emphasize efficiency, create routines that emphasize formality, and create business practices that emphasize dedication to clients. By moving the focus from how employees look to what they do, workplaces can become more intentional and more effective at accomplishing the organization's goal.

Gender-Neutral as Default

We recommend that workplaces offer all employees the option to list their preferred name and pronouns if they so desire, to be used in all workplace environments where legal information is not required. By introducing this option, organizations increase the visibility of an aspect of workplace life that most employees take for granted, and give trans employees the option to more easily disclose name or pronoun preferences that might otherwise be difficult to bring up.

We recommend, additionally, that HR departments suggest to their managers to use the gender-neutral singular pronoun "they" in reference to all employees unless otherwise specified. This is a difficult recommendation in many respects, primary being that it directly challenges a habit almost every adult person has learned—automatically gendering the people they see. It is something that we learn from early childhood—people with long hair should be addressed by "she" and people with short hair should be addressed by "he"; people with deep voices are "he" and people with high voices are "she"—and almost never question. These assumptions, however, negatively affect all people whose appearances do not fall within the arbitrary categories of "man" and "woman": women with flat chests who have had mastectomies, women of color with heavy body hair, men who apply makeup, nonbinary trans people, and many, many others. As many of our interviewees described, the experience of having one's gender invalidated through the wrong gender pronoun, especially when done consistently, is exhausting. Reasserting and recorrecting the same information, day after day, is a significant psychological and emotional tax on all those who don't conform to binary gender norms.

The solution is simple: treat gender like we treat a characteristic like religious beliefs—specify only if and when the information is known. By asking managers to use the gender-neutral "they" as default, we give employees the agency to have their identities communicated and validated in the workplace. This recommendation would not have managers use "they" for all employees, at all times—rather, it would ask that managers simply not assume, and use a pronoun like "he" or "she" only after knowing that these pronouns are appropriate. For people whose pronouns are often assumed incorrectly, such a practice potentially has a huge positive effect on their perception of workplace acceptance. By taking gender-neutral as default and modeling it with supervisors and managers, organizations can push their workplaces toward greater trans-inclusivity.

Education and Training

Organizations looking to become more trans-inclusive must understand that for many trans people—indeed, many people regardless of whether or not they are trans—having their gender identities and expressions validated in the workplace is of high importance. Thus, creating a workplace environment where such respect is commonplace and learned by all employees is of high importance as well. A workplace with otherwise perfect trans-inclusivity policy must still grapple with creating a culture of respect in which trans employees can thrive—no easy task, especially if the workplace or organization has a deeply entrenched or traditional workplace culture that cannot easily integrate trans people. Even the most dedicated organizational leader and the most committed workplace will make mistakes on the path to inclusivity; even the most committed ally can accidentally misgender or exclude a trans person.

With this in mind, *we recommend that HR departments and specialists take on the responsibility of creating a trans-inclusive workplace culture through trainings, educational efforts, and other events; communicate with trans employees; and work to resolve conflicts as they arise without the use of harsh discipline.* A reconciliatory and growth-minded approach to trans-inclusivity can convey the urgency of trans-inclusivity without provoking as much backlash or resentment among employees as a more authoritative, disciplinary approach would. Perhaps more importantly, taking a more cooperative rather than punitive approach to education addresses the reality that, for many people, trans discrimination comes not out of malicious attempts at doing harm but instead out of learned fear, suspicion, or distrust. Many employees who act in transphobic or exclusionary ways may do so because it is what they were taught to do in the environments they were socialized in, or because they have internalized prejudices from those around them that they are not even aware of.

Framing trans-inclusivity as a goal of an entire organization or workplace is a strong first step in creating inclusive cultures, and can be a powerful, yet understanding approach to helping even the most prejudiced members of an organization become more inclusive. When this approach is paired with other existing protections like nondiscrimination policy, formalized procedures for on-the-job transition, and access to proper facilities, organizations can move intentionally, yet gently toward trans-inclusivity while still protecting and valuing their trans employees.

Which educational efforts should HR focus on first? The answer varies, depending on the organization: different trainings will have different impacts on different workplaces. For corporations with an HR department, these personnel are an obvious choice for receiving training. If HR is unfamiliar with trans people or does not know how to coordinate inclusivity efforts across the organization, trans-inclusivity is heavily hindered in the workplace. *We recommend that all HR departments partner with local and/or national-level trans organizations—or trans employees, as is convenient with available resources—to create specialized agendas to make their organizations more trans-inclusive.* With this direction, HR is more able to take the lead of trans-inclusivity across the organization. *We recommend, additionally, that HR work with trans organizations to both create and give trainings, such that recipients of these trainings are familiarized with trans people and given the appropriate language to interact with them.* Often times, inadvertent harm done to trans employees happens because people are unfamiliar with trans people, and may not know how to interact with them respectfully. Employees often heavily question trans employees on personal and private parts of their lives, which both takes time away from productive work and can make trans employees feel anxious, tense, or marginalized. Such trainings can make employees more comfortable around trans people and more able to effectively collaborate with trans employees on workplace-related matters without unnecessary or invasive questioning.

These trainings can be focused toward different organizational audiences, depending on the type of organization and the immediate situation where training is needed.

In workplaces and organizations where managers play a large role in employee life, a trans-inclusive or trans-friendly manager can potentially have a huge impact on a trans employee's workplace experience—even in workplaces without strong cultures of inclusivity. Offering training to managers in these organizations can maximize the impact of training conducted with either limited resources or a massive number of employees. *We recommend that managers be educated on common issues trans people face in workplaces, and be strongly encouraged to model inclusive behavior at work like using trans employees' desired name and pronouns and including trans people in community-building activities.*

In smaller organizations and workplaces, especially those where managers or supervisors have limited influence over employees' workplace experiences, it can be more effective to focus on offering training to all employees who directly work with a trans employee. When a trans employee's day at work involves heavy communication or interaction with other employees in the workplace, focusing on making these interactions less stressful for trans employees can be the most effective use of resources. *We recommend that in organizations where intra-organization communication is common, employees all be educated on trans-inclusive language and best practices to increase workplace productivity.*

In general, many people possess the desire to be supportive and friendly to trans people, yet do not have the knowledge or vocabulary to back up their intentions. For these reasons, many employees inadvertently insult, marginalize, or exclude trans people in their speech or actions. Employees may not understand that what to them seem like minor or even inconsequential actions can be as harmful as they are to trans people. As Taylor, a 34-year-old trans woman explains, " 'him,' 'she/him,' 'sir,' that bothers me worse than 'fuck you bitch, tranny whore' or whatever . . . pronoun usage, wrong pronoun usage is much more hurtful to me than curse words."

Employers and coworkers who may not have explicit transphobic beliefs can nevertheless marginalize and hurt trans employees.*Thus, we recommend that all trans-specific trainings directly link experiences of discrimination to the impact they have on trans employees.* By focusing more on the link between discrimination and impact, organizations also make their employee training programs more directly applicable to the workplace, increase employees' understanding of other people, and improve workplace relationships. Many employees are often surprised to know that misgendering or jokes cause trans people much harm, because the harm that is caused is often hidden or endured by trans employees. By making the impact of marginalizing language known in the workplace, organizations can begin to foster cultures of respect and inclusivity.

Limiting Information

Especially in workplaces that are moving toward trans-inclusivity but not quite there yet, knowledge of an employee's trans identity can make that employee a target for discrimination, especially in job interviews. Sam, a white and Latinx butch woman in their thirties, shared with us a story of obvious hiring discrimination when their interviewer took stock of their gender-diverse appearance. "One person I interviewed with, she liked me, and [wanted me] to meet . . . [her] boss . . . she walks out, brings him in and I can just see immediately his face change the instant he registers who I am . . . so he's like rushing through the interview and is dismissing me, and I could just tell within the minute he was done with me." Many participants reported similar experiences—some interviewees talked about being denied jobs due to interviewers being put off by their appearances, the pitch of their voices, or even knowledge of past job where they had used different pronouns.

In most of these cases, information about gender identity and appearance is wholly unnecessary to evaluate job competence. *We recommend that HR departments reorganize interview criteria to reflect only those characteristics that might impact the job or task interviewed for and to carefully design the interview process to be blind to all unnecessary criteria.* For example, organizations working in manufacturing can hire employees solely on the basis of their skill and proficiency at a range of tasks. We can imagine an interview process where an interviewee performs these tasks, is assigned a number or identification code, and then has their results (thus anonymized) evaluated. For many jobs, these identity-blind interview methods would drastically increase all diversity in hired employees, not just for trans people. *We recommend, additionally, that organizations seriously consider lowering the frequency with which phone interviews are used due to the many subconscious judgments that interviewers often make based on a nontask-relevant characteristic like voice tone and pitch.* Many interviewees expressed anxiety over phone interviews, and shared experiences of being denied for a job due to interviewers' concerns or confusion over their voices.

We recommend that all interviewers who meet with trans people face-to-face be trained to evaluate candidates only on the basis of the evaluation criteria relevant to the job, and that HR departments regularly offer implicit bias training to these interviewers. Targeting interviewer bias is a concrete step many organizations can take to address a lack of diversity in employee populations.

Hiring practices are not the only place where organizations can work to limit unnecessary information. Anonymizing candidate/interviewee data is also a crucial way to support trans employees when promotion is on the table. Alex, a white trans woman in her forties, told us a story of a senior-level employee in her workplace who transitioned on the job. This employee was on track for a vice president position, but upon transitioning saw her career stagnate. Alex told us that this transition was a "career killer" for this employee, and that witnessing these experience discouraged Alex—herself a senior-level employee—from transitioning at work. She eventually quit her job due to stress. *We recommend that organizations formalize promotion criteria (rather than relying on metrics like "likability" or "professionalism"), make the promoting process as transparent as possible to candidates, and anonymize candidate information to evaluators and those who otherwise determine promotion.* These changes will ideally make the promotion process as merit-based as possible, and give trans employees a fighting chance at moving past entry-level jobs.

Some workplaces may find that their desired changes to workplace culture are not progressing as quickly as they would like, and seek faster solutions to take care of their trans employees as best as they can. Some workplaces may have transphobic managers or supervisors, while others may have transphobic or prejudiced employees. For example, Blake, a 26-year-old trans man, began to face discrimination at his workplace only after his district manager found out that he was trans by looking through old paperwork. *We recommend that HR assume ownership of hiring documents and other documents with sensitive information, otherwise restricting direct supervisors from accessing this information unless explicitly required.* Had Blake's trans status not been outed to his manager, he might have been able to maintain a positive relationship and would not have quit his job.

Safe and Accessible Bathrooms

For many trans employees, bathrooms are a recurring and constant source of stress and anxiety. Bathrooms are often places where trans people come under the most scrutiny, and are most policed for having gender expressions or appearances that do not conform to people's expectations of what "men" and "women" should look like. For these reasons, bathrooms can often be dangerous and potentially traumatic spaces for trans employees, many of whom cope by using bathrooms during inopportune times, using bathrooms only when they are empty, or even refusing to use bathrooms in the workplace at all. Many nontrans people are only beginning to realize the intense addition burden that unsafe bathroom situations create for trans people, but much work still remains to be done regarding creating inclusive and accessible bathrooms for trans employees. Improving the bathroom situation for trans employees removes a significant amount of anxiety that many trans employees hold around workplaces, and better allows trans employees to perform to their full potential on the job.

For those employees who feel uncomfortable in or are excluded from both men's and women's bathrooms, particularly gender-neutral, genderqueer, or otherwise nonbinary trans people, additional bathroom facilities can be game-changing. Many workplaces already have these facilities in the form of single-stall staff bathrooms, but these bathrooms are often poorly maintained, locked, or otherwise forgotten about. *We recommend that organizations add at least one single-stall, all-gender bathroom in every workplace, and that such bathrooms be regularly maintained and cleaned to the same standard as other bathrooms.* We understand that many organizations often lack the funding and resources to create additional bathrooms on sites in which such infrastructure is lacking. *We additionally recommend that organizations seriously consider de-gendering at least one set of binary-gendered bathrooms in the workplace, and making them into multi-stall, all-gender inclusive bathrooms.*

We do not make this recommendation lightly—such a move is likely to be controversial, as it challenges deeply entrenched beliefs people may hold about men, women, and gender segregation. People may believe that allowing men into the same bathrooms as women is an unnecessarily risky and dangerous move. They may be concerned about the sexual assault, peeping, or harassment that all-gender bathrooms might enable. Or, perhaps, they may simply be uncomfortable without knowing a clear reason why—"men belong here" and "women belong there," we might say, and stop at that. What we are worried about, in other words, is the very real misogyny that despite our best efforts persists in organizations across the country and around the world, and the risks of giving that misogyny an opportunity to do harm within all-gender bathrooms. With this in mind, we must strongly assert that our recommendations for a more trans-inclusive workplace must be considered and pursued in tandem with other efforts toward gender parity and equity at work; neither effort can replace the necessity of the other.

Can workplaces create a culture of mutual respect such that all-gender bathrooms could exist without anxiety? We believe it is possible—and for many trans employees, essential. What trans employees need, at the end of the day, is not only inclusive structures and facilities but inclusive workplace cultures that accept, include, and validate their identities, experiences, and needs. Without this culture, trans employees may not even feel safe enough to use facilities that include them—like Blake, a 26-year-old trans man who "was too scared [to use the men's room]. There are definitely people there that I knew would not be okay if for some reason a lock didn't work." Because Blake was afraid he might be exposed to transphobic harassment, his manager bent the rules for Blake and allowed him to use the bathrooms when not officially on break. While this instance of a supportive manager salvaged Blake's experience at this workplace, had the workplace culture been more explicitly trans-friendly, this manager's support would not have been necessary for Blake to be able to meet such a basic need as bathroom usage at work.

PARTING WORDS

From the extensive interviews we carried out, we learned a wealth of information about the pervasive and daunting discrimination faced by trans employees across a multitude of industries and workplaces. We heard stories of prejudice, loss, and exhaustion—and also stories of resilience, survival, creativity, and grit. It has long been clear that discrimination is a problem that plagues many organizations, even ones that position themselves against it. What we need now is not a call to action, but a plan for action, a concrete list of actionable changes, goals, and reimaginings for organizations to take on.

It is our hope that these recommendations we have provided add to the national and international conversations already happening for equity and justice for trans people. The hard work of lobbying, advocating, and policy making lies ahead, but we are confident in the strength of the trans community, and optimistic about the integrity of cisgender allies who fight for it. In this book, we have dedicated an entire chapter to those strategies trans employees use to avoid discrimination in the workplace. While we continue to be amazed and humbled by the stories we have heard, it is our honest hope that, someday, trans employees will no longer need these strategies. That someday, trans people and trans communities can secure economic well-being—and the political, social, religious, and cultural liberation that must accompany it.

Bibliography

Acker, Joan. 1990. "Hierarchies, Jobs, Bodies: A Theory of Gendered Organizations." *Gender and Society* 4(2): 139–158.

American Psychiatric Association. 2013. *Diagnostic and Statistical Manual of Mental Disorders* (5th ed.). Arlington, VA: American Psychiatric Publishing.

Badgett, M. V. Lee. 1995. "The Wage Effects of Sexual Orientation Discrimination." *Industrial & Labor Relations Review* 48(4): 726–739.

Benjamin, Harry. 1969. "Newer Aspects of the Transsexual Phenomenon." *Journal of Sex Research* 5(2): 135–141.

Blair, Irene V., and Mahzarin R. Banaji. 1996. "Automatic and Controlled Processes in Stereotype Priming." *Journal of Personality and Social Psychology* 70: 1142–1163.

Bornstein, Kate. 1994. *Gender Outlaw: On Men, Women, and the Rest of Us.* New York: Routledge.

Boswell, Holly. 1991. "The Transgender Alternative." *Chrysalis Quarterly* 1(2): 29–31.

Boyd, Nan Alamilla. 1999. "The Materiality of Gender: Looking for Lesbian Bodies in Transgender History." *Journal of Lesbian Studies* 3(3): 73–81.

Brescoll, Victoria L., and Eric L. Uhlmann. 2005. "Attitudes toward Traditional and Nontraditional Parents." *Psychology of Women Quarterly* 29(4): 436–445.

Brewer, Marilynn, and Layton Lui. 1989. "The Primacy of Age and Sex in the Structure of Person Categories." *Social Cognition* 7(3): 262–274.

Browne, Kath. 2004. "Genderism and the Bathroom Problem: (Re)Materialising Sexed Sites, (Re)Creating Sexed Bodies." *Gender, Place, and Culture* 11(3): 331–346.

Butler, Judith. 1993. *Bodies That Matter.* New York: Routledge.

Callahan, Joan. 2009. "Same-Sex Marriage: Why It Matters—At Least for Now." *Hypatia* 24(1): 70–80.

Carli, Linda L., Suzanne LaFleur, and Christopher C. Loeber. 1995. "Nonverbal Behavior, Gender, and Influence." *Journal of Personality and Social Psychology* 68: 1030–1041.

Ceperich, Sherry D., and Kristina M. Hash. 2006. "Workplace Issues." In *Sexual Orientation & Gender Expression in Social Work Practice: Working with Gay, Lesbian, Bisexual, and Transgender People* (pp. 405–426), edited by D. F. Morrow and L. Messinger. New York: Columbia University Press.

Coleman, Eli, et al. 2012. "Standards of Care for the Health of Transsexual, Transgender, and Gender-nonconforming People, Version 7." *International Journal of Transgenderism* 13(4): 165–232.

Connell, Catherine, and Kristen Schilt. 2007. "Do Workplace Gender Transitions Make Gender Trouble?" *Gender, Work & Organization* 14(6): 596–618.

Connell, R. W. 1987. *Gender and Power: Society, the Person and Sexual Politics.* Redwood City, CA: Stanford University Press.

Connell, R. W. 1996. "Teaching the Boys: New Research on Masculinity, and Gender Strategies for Schools." *The Teachers College Record* 98(2): 206–235.

Connell, R. W. 2005. "Masculinities." Oakland, CA: University of California Press.

Connell, R.W. 2009. "Accountable Conduct: 'Doing Gender' in Transsexual and Political Retrospect." *Gender and Society* 23(1): 104–111.

Connell, R.W. 2010. "Two Cans of Paint: A Transsexual Life Story, with Reflections on Gender Change and History." *Sexualities* 13(1): 3–19.

Connell, R. W., and James W. Messerschmidt. 2005. "Hegemonic Masculinity: Rethinking the Concept." *Gender & Society,* 19: 829–859.

Cook, S. W. 1978. "Interpersonal and Attitudinal Outcomes in Cooperating Interracial Groups." *Journal of Research and Development in Education* 12: 97–113.

Cook, S. W. 1984. "Cooperative Interaction in Multiethnic Contexts." In *Groups in Contact: The Psychology of Desegregation* (pp. 155–185), edited by N. Miller and M. B. Brewer. Orlando, FL: Academic Press.

Craig, Traci, and Jessica LaCroix. 2011. "Tomboy as Protective Identity." *Journal of Lesbian Studies* 15(4): 450–465.

Cromwell, Jason. 1994. "Default Assumptions or the Billy Tipton Phenomenon." *FTM Newsletter* 28: 4–5.

Day, Nancy E., and Patricia Schoenrade. 1997. "Staying in the Closet versus Coming Out: Relationships between Communication about Sexual Orientation and Work Attitudes." *Personnel Psychology* 50: 157–161.

Deaux, Kay, and Mary Kite. 1993. "Gender Stereotypes." In *Psychology of Women: A Handbook of Issues and Theories* (pp. 107–139), edited by F. L. Denmark and M. A. Paludi. Westport, CT: Greenwood Press.

Demetriou, D. Z. 2001. "Connell's Concept of Hegemonic Masculinity: A Critique." *Theory and Society* 30(3): 337–361.

Derlega, Valerian J., and Alan L. Chaikin. 1976. "Norms Affecting Self-disclosure in Men and Women." *Journal of Consulting and Clinical Psychology* 44(3): 376–380.

Dijker, A. J., and W. Koomen. 2003. "Extending Weiner's Attribution-Emotion Model of Stigmatization of Ill Persons." *Basic and Applied Social Psychology* 25(1): 51–68.

Dozier, Raine. 2005. "Beards, Breasts, and Bodies: Doing Sex in a Gendered World." *Gender and Society* 19(3): 297–316.

Dreger, Alice Domurat. 1998. " 'Ambiguous Sex'—or Ambivalent Medicine?: Ethical Issues in the Treatment of Intersexuality." *Hastings Center Report* 28(3): 24–35.

Duberman, Martin B., Martha Vicinus, and George Chauncey. 1989. *Hidden from History: Reclaiming the Gay and Lesbian Past*. New York: New American Library.

Eagly, Alice H. 1987. *Sex Differences in Social Behavior: A Social-Role Interpretation*. Hillsdale, NJ: Erlbaum.

Eagly, Alice H., Mona G. Makhijani, and Bruce G. Klonsky. 1992. "Gender and the Evaluation of Leaders: A Meta-analysis." *Psychological Bulletin* 111(1): 3–22.

Eagly, Alice H., and Steven J. Karau. 2002. "Role Congruity Theory of Prejudice toward Female Leaders." *Psychological Review* 109(3): 573–598.

Eagly, Alice H., and Linda L. Carli. 2007. *Through the Labyrinth: The Truth about How Women Become Leaders*. Boston, MA: Harvard Business School Press.

England, Paula. 1992. *Comparable Worth: Theories and Evidence*. New York: Aldine De Gruyter.

Fausto-Sterling, Anne. 2000. *Sexing the Body*. New York: Basic Books.

Fenstermaker, Sarah, Candace West, and Don Zimmerman. 2002. "Gender Inequality: New Conceptual Terrain." In *Doing Gender, Doing Difference: Inequality, Power, and Institutional Change* (pp. 25–39). New York: Routledge.

Franklin, Karen. 2000. "Antigay Behaviors among Young Adults Prevalence, Patterns, and Motivators in a Noncriminal Population." *Journal of Interpersonal Violence* 15(4): 339–362.

Gagné, Patricia, and Richard Tewksbury. 1998. "Conformity Pressures and Gender Resistance among Transgendered Individuals." *Social Problems* 45(1): 81–101.

Gagné, Patricia, Richard Tewksbury, and Deanna McGaughey. 1997. "Coming Out and Crossing Over: Identity Formation and Proclamation in a Transgender Community." *Gender and Society* 11(4): 478–508.

Garfinkel, Harold. 1967. *Studies in Ethnomethodology.* Englewood Cliffs, NJ: Prentice Hall.

Goffman, E. 1963. *Stigma: Notes on the Management of Spoiled Identity.* Englewood Cliffs, NJ: Prentice-Hall.

Gorham-Rowan, Mary, and Richard Morris. 2006. "Aerodynamic Analysis of Male-to-Female Transgender Voice." *Journal of Voice* 20(2): 251–262.

Grant, Jaime M., Lisa A. Mottet, Justin Tanis, Jack Harrison, Jody L. Herman, and Mara Keisling. 2011. *Injustice at Every Turn: A Report of the National Transgender Discrimination Survey.* National Center for Transgender Equality and National Gay and Lesbian Task Force. Washington, DC.

Hagen, Randi L., and Arnold Kahn. 1975. "Discrimination against Competent Women." *Journal of Applied Social Psychology* 5(4): 362–376.

Halberstam, Judith. 2002. "The Good, the Bad, the Ugly: Men, Women, and Masculinity." In *Masculinity Studies and Feminist Theory* (pp. 344–367), edited by Judith Kegan Gardiner. New York: Columbia University Press.

Harrison, Jack, Jaime Grant, and Jody L. Herman. 2012. "A Gender Not Listed Here: Genderqueers, Gender Rebels, and OtherWise in the National Transgender Discrimination Survey." *LGBTQ Public Policy Journal at the Harvard Kennedy School* 2(1): 13–24.

Heilman, Madeline E. 2001. "Description and Prescription: How Gender Stereotypes Prevent Women's Ascent up the Organizational Ladder." *Journal of Social Issues* 57: 657–674.

Heilman, Madeline E., Aaron S. Wallen, Daniella Fuchs, and Melinda M. Tamkins. 2004. "Penalties for Success: Reactions to Women Who Succeed at Male Gender-Typed Tasks." *Journal of Applied Psychology* 89: 416–427.

Herdt, Gilbert H. 1994. *Third Sex, Third Gender: Beyond Sexual Dimorphism in Culture and History.* New York: Zone Books.

Huang, L., A. D. Galinsky, D. H. Gruenfeld, and L. E. Guillory. 2011. "Powerful Postures versus Powerful Roles: Which Is the Proximate Correlate of Thought and Behavior?" *Psychological Science* 22(1): 95–102.

James, S. E., J. L. Herman, S. Rankin, M. Keisling, L. Mottet, and M. A. Anafi. 2016. "The Report of the 2015 US Transgender Survey." Washington, DC: National Center for Transgender Equality.

Johnson, Kerri L., Jonathan B. Freeman, and Kristin Pauker. 2012. "Race Is Gendered: How Covarying Phenotypes and Stereotypes Bias Sex Categorization." *Journal of Personality and Social Psychology*, 102: 116–131.

Jones, Jordy. 1994. "FTM Crossdresser Murdered." *FTM Newsletter* 26(3).

Kanter, Rosabeth Moss. 1977. *Men and Women of the Corporation*. New York: Basic Books.

Katz, Jonathan. 1976. "Passing Women." *Gay American History: Lesbian and Gay Men in the U.S.A.: A Documentary*. New York: Crowell.

Kimmel, Michael S. 1994. "Masculinity as Homophobia: Fear, Shame, and Silence in the Construction of Gender Identity." In *Research on Men and Masculinities Series: Theorizing Masculinities* (pp. 119–142), edited by H. Brod and M. Kaufman. Thousand Oaks, CA: Sage Publications, Inc.

Kricheli-Katz, Tamar. 2012. "Choice, Discrimination, and the Motherhood Penalty." *Law & Society Review* 46(3): 557–587.

Kricheli-Katz, Tamar. 2013. "Choice-Based Discrimination: Labor-Force-Type Discrimination against Gay Men, the Obese, and Mothers." *Journal of Empirical Legal Studies* 10(4): 670–695.

Levitt, Heidi M., and Katherine R. Hiestand. 2004. "A Quest for Authenticity: Contemporary Butch Gender." *Sex Roles* 50: 605–621.

Lorah, Peggy, and Shanti M. Pepper. 2008. "Career Issues and Workplace Considerations for the Transsexual Community: Bridging a Gap of Knowledge for Career Counselors and Mental Health Care Providers." *The Career Development Quarterly*, 56: 334–338.

Love, Heather. 2014. "Queer." *Transgender Studies Quarterly* 1: 172–176.

Lyness, Karen S., and Michael K. Judiesch. 1999. "Are Women More Likely to Be Hired or Promoted into Management Positions?" *Journal of Vocational Behavior* 54: 158–173.

Meyer, Ilan H. 2003. "Prejudice, Social Stress, and Mental Health in Lesbian, Gay, and Bisexual Populations: Conceptual Issues and Research Evidence." *Psychological Bulletin* 129(5): 674–697.

Meyerson, Debra, and Megan Tompkins. 2007. "Tempered Radicals as Institutional Change Agents: The Case of Advancing Gender Equity at the University of Michigan." *Harvard Journal of Law and Gender* 30: 303–322.

Money, John, Joan G. Hampson, and John L. Hampson. 1955. "Hermaphroditism: Recommendations Concerning Assignment of Sex, Change of Sex and Psychologic Management." *Bulletin of the Johns Hopkins Hospital* 97(4): 284–300.

Monro, Surya. 2007. "Transmuting Gender Binaries: The Theoretical Challenge." *Sociological Research Online* 12(1).

Moss-Racusin, Corinne A., Julie E. Phelan, and Laurie A. Rudman. 2010. "When Men Break the Gender Rules: Status Incongruity and Backlash against Modest Men." *Psychology of Men & Masculinity* 11(2): 140–151.

Nestle, J., C. Howell, and R. A. Wilchins (Eds.). 2002. *Genderqueer: Voices from beyond the Sexual Binary.* New York: Alyson Publications.

Neumann, Kerstin, and Cornelia Welzel. 2004. "The Importance of the Voice in Male-to-Female Transsexualism." *Journal of Voice* 18(1): 153–167.

Olian, Judy D., Donald P. Schwab, and Yitchak Haberfeld. 1988. "The Impact of Applicant Gender Compared to Qualifications on Hiring Recommendations: A Meta-Analysis of Experimental Studies." *Organizational Behavior and Human Decision Processes* 41: 180–195.

Padavic, Irene, and Barbara Reskin. 2002. *Women and Men at Work,* 2nd ed. Thousand Oaks, CA: Pine Forge Press.

Paluck, E. L. and D. P. Green. 2009. "Prejudice Reduction: What Works? A Review and Assessment of Research and Practice." *Annual Review of Psychology* 60: 339–367.

Pascoe, Cheri Jo. 2005. " 'Dude, You're a Fag': Adolescent Masculinity and the Fag Discourse." *Sexualities* 8(3): 329–346.

Phelan, Julie E., Corinne A. Moss-Racusin, and Laurie A. Rudman. 2008. "Competent yet Out in the Cold: Shifting Hiring Criteria Reflects Backlash toward Agentic Women." *Psychology of Women Quarterly* 32: 406–413.

Quinn, Diane M., and Stephanie R. Chaudoir. 2009. "Living with a Concealable Stigmatized Identity: The Impact of Anticipated Stigma, Centrality, Salience, and Cultural Stigma on Psychological Distress and Health." *Journal of Personality and Social Psychology* 97 (4): 634–651.

Ridgeway, Cecilia L. 2001. "Gender, Status, and Leadership." *Journal of Social Issues* 57: 637–655.

Ridgeway, Cecilia L., and Shelley J. Correll. 2004. "Unpacking the Gender System: A Theoretical Perspective on Gender Beliefs and Social Relations." *Gender and Society* 18(4): 510–531.

Risman, Barbara. 1998. *Gender Vertigo: American Families in Transition.* New Haven, CT: Yale University Press.

Rivers, Ian. 2001. "The Bullying of Sexual Minorities at School: Its Nature and Long-term Correlates." *Educational and Child Psychology* 18(1): 32–46.

Robinson, S. L., and R. J. Bennett. 1995. "A Typology of Deviant Workplace Behaviors: A Multidimensional Scaling Study." *Academy of Management Journal* 38: 555–572.

Rodin, Miriam, Judy Price, Francisco Sanchez, and Sharel McElligot. 1989. "Derogation, Exclusion, and Unfair Treatment of Persons with Social Flaws: Controllability of Stigma and the Attribution of Prejudice." *Personality and Social Psychology Bulletin* 15(3): 439–451.

Roen, Katrina. 2001. "Of Right Bodies and Wrong Bodies: The Forging of Corpus Transsexualis through Discursive Manoeuvre and Surgical Manipulation." *International Journal of Critical Psychology* 3: 9–121.

Rudman, Laurie A. 1998. "Self-Promotion as a Risk Factor for Women: The Costs and Benefits of Counterstereotypical Impression Management." *Journal of Personality and Social Psychology* 74: 629–645.

Rudman, Laurie A., and Peter Glick. 1999. "Feminized Management and Backlash toward Agentic Women: The Hidden Costs to Women of a Kinder, Gentler Image of Middle Managers." *Journal of Personality and Social Psychology* 77: 1004–1010.

Rudman, Laurie A., and Peter Glick. 2001. "Prescriptive Gender Stereotypes and Backlash toward Agentic Women." *Journal of Social Issues* 57: 743–762.

Rudman, Laurie A., Corrinne A. Moss-Racusin, Julie E. Phelan, and Sanne Nauts. 2012. "Status Incongruity and Backlash Effects: Defending the Gender Hierarchy Motivates Prejudice against Female Leaders." *Journal of Experimental Social Psychology* 48(1): 165–179.

Schilt, Kristen. 2006. "Just One of the Guys? How Transmen Make Gender Visible at Work." *Gender and Society* 20(4): 465–490.

Schilt, Kristen. 2010. *Just One of the Guys?: Transgender Men and the Persistence of Gender Inequality.* University of Chicago Press.

Schilt, Kristen, and Laurel Westbrook. 2009. "Doing Gender, Doing Heteronormativity, 'Gender Normals,' Transgender People, and the Social Maintenance of Heterosexuality." *Gender and Society* 23(4): 440–464.

Schilt, Kristen, and Matthew Wiswall. 2008. "Before and After: Gender Transitions, Human Capital, and Workplace Experiences." *The B.E. Journal of Economic Analysis and Policy* 8(1): 1–28.

Schippers, Mimi. 2007. "Recovering the Feminine Other: Masculinity, Femininity, and Gender Hegemony." *Theory and Society* 36(1): 85–102.

Stangor, Charles, Laure Lynch, Changming Duan, and Beth Glass. 1992. "Categorization of Individuals on the Basis of Multiple Social Features." *Journal of Personality and Social Psychology* 62: 207–218.

Stryker, Susan. 1995. "Local Transsexual History." *TNT: Transsexual News Telegraph* 5: 14–15.

Stryker, Susan. 2008. *Transgender History.* Berkeley, CA: Seal Press.

Stryker, Susan. 2011. "The Time Has Come to Think about Gayle Rubin." *GLQ: A Journal of Lesbian and Gay Studies* 17(1): 79–83.

Tompkins, Avery. 2014. "Asterisk." *TSQ: Transgender Studies Quarterly* 1: 26–27.

Transgender Law Center. 2006. "Good Jobs NOW! A Snapshot of the Economic Health of San Francisco's Transgender Communities." San Francisco: Transgender Law Center.

Transgender Law Center. 2009. *The State of Transgender California Report.* San Francisco: Transgender Law Center.

Van Borsel, John, Joke Janssens, and Marc De Bodt. 2009. "Breathiness as a Feminine Voice Characteristic: A Perceptual Approach." *Journal of Voice* 23(3): 291–294.

Wålinder, Jan. 1968. "Transsexualism: Definition, Prevalence and Sex Distribution." *Acta Psychiatrica Scandinavica* 43(203): 255–258.

Weiner, Bernard. 1995. *Judgments of Responsibility: A Foundation for a Theory of Social Conduct*. New York: Guilford Press.

Weiner, Bernard, Raymond P. Perry, and Jamie Magnusson. 1988. "An Attributional Analysis of Reactions to Stigmas." *Journal of Personality and Social Psychology* 55(5): 738–748.

West, Candace, and Don H. Zimmerman. 1987. "Doing Gender." *Gender & Society* 1(2): 125–151.

Westbrook, Laurel, and Kristen Schilt. 2013. "Doing Gender, Determining Gender: Transgender People, Gender Panics, and the Maintenance of the Sex/Gender/Sexuality System." *Gender and Society* 23: 440–464.

Wilchins, Riki Anne. 1995. "What's in a Name? The Politics of Gender Speak." *Transgender Tapestry* 74: 46–77.

Wiley, Mary Glen, and Arlene Eskilson. 1985. "Speech Style, Gender Stereotypes, and Corporate Success: What If Women Talk More Like Men?" *Sex Roles* 12: 993–1007.

Willer, Robb, Christabel Rogalin, Bridget Conlon, and Michael T. Wojnowicz. 2013. "Overdoing Gender: A Test of the Masculine Overcompensation Thesis." *American Journal of Sociology* 118(4): 980–1022.

Williams, Christine L. 1992. "The Glass Escalator: Hidden Advantages for Men in the 'Female' Professions." *Social Problems* 39(3): 253–267.

Williams, John E., and Deborah L. Best. 1982. *Measuring Sex Stereotypes: A Thirty-nation Study*. Beverly Hills, CA: Sage Publications, Inc.

Wong, Paul T. P., Gail Kettlewell, and C. F. Sproule. 1985. "On the Importance of Being Masculine: Sex Role, Attribution, and Women's Career Achievement." *Sex Roles* 12: 757–769.

Yoder, Janice D. 1994. "Looking beyond Numbers: The Effects of Gender Status, Job Prestige and Occupational Gender-Typing on Tokenism Processes." *Social Psychology Quarterly* 57: 150–159.

Yoshino, K. 2006. *Covering: The Hidden Assault on Our Civil Rights*. New York: Random House.

Zillmann, D. 1991. "Empathy: Affect from Bearing Witness to the Emotions of Others." In *Responding to the Screen: Reception and Reaction Processes* (pp. 135–167), edited by J. Bryant and D. Zillmann. Hillsdale, NJ: Lawrence Erlbaum Associates.

Zimman, Lal. 2013. "Hegemonic Masculinity and the Variability of Gay-sounding Speech: The Perceived Sexuality of Transgender Men." *Journal of Language and Sexuality* 2(1): 1–39.

Index

ABOUT THE AUTHORS

Alison Ash Fogarty, PhD, is a sociologist, sexual empowerment coach and educator, and founder of TurnON.love. She is committed to community-building to promote empathy and acceptance across a spectrum of human experiences. She investigates the complex social challenges that often lead to disempowering sexual experiences and romantic relationships. Fogarty has coauthored articles published in the *American Journal of Sociology* and *Gender & Society*, as well as several chapters in academic anthologies. As a champion for others engaging in radical self-exploration and courageous self-expression, she offers coaching for individuals and couples and teaches courses and workshops designed to provide the necessary but rarely taught tools we need to thrive in intimacy. She earned her doctorate at Stanford University.

Lily Zheng is a design researcher with Stanford University's Diversity and First-Generation Office. A writer and activist whose work has been featured in the *New York Times, Psychology Today,* and *Stanford Politics,* Zheng speaks around the world on topics of social justice, transgender inclusion, and sexuality. In her role as a diversity and inclusion consultant and transgender advocate, she works with organizations to turn positive intent into positive impact through inclusive policy, innovative practice, and intergroup communication. She earned her master's degree in sociology at Stanford University.